CLASSIC SERMONS

ON

CHRISTIAN SERVICE

CLASSIC SERMONS Series

CLASSIC SERMONS

ON

CHRISTIAN SERVICE

Compiled by
Warren W. Wiersbe

HENDRICKSON PUBLISHERS

CLASSIC SERMONS
ON
CHRISTIAN SERVICE

CONTENTS

PREFACE

THE *KREGEL CLASSIC SERMONS SERIES* is an attempt to assemble and publish meaningful sermons from master preachers about significant themes.

These are *sermons*, not essays or chapters taken from books about themes. Not all of these sermons could be called "great," but all of them are *meaningful*. They apply the truths of the Bible to the needs of the human heart, which is something that all effective preaching must do.

While some are better known than others, all of the preachers, whose sermons I have selected, had important ministries and were highly respected in their day. The fact that a sermon is included in this volume does not mean that either the compiler or the publisher agrees with or endorses everything that the man did, preached, or wrote. The sermon is here because it has a valued contribution to make.

These are sermons about *significant* themes. The pulpit is no place to play with trivia. The preacher has thirty minutes in which to help mend broken hearts, change defeated lives, and save lost souls; and he can never accomplish this demanding ministry by distributing homiletical tid-bits. In these difficult days, we do not need "clever" pulpiteers who discuss the times; we need dedicated ambassadors who will preach the eternities.

The reading of these sermons can enrich your own spiritual life. The studying of them can enrich your own skills as an interpreter and expounder of God's truth. However God uses these sermons in your own life and ministry, my prayer is that His Church around the world will be encouraged and strengthened.

WARREN W. WIERSBE

Our Motto

Charles Haddon Spurgeon (1834-1892) is undoubtedly the most famous minister of modern times. Converted in 1850, he united with the Baptists and very soon began to preach in various places. He became pastor of the Baptist church in Waterbeach in 1851, and 3 years later he was called to the decaying Park Street Church, London. Within a short time, the work began to prosper, a new church was built and dedicated in 1861, and Spurgeon became London's most popular preacher. In 1855 he began to publish his sermons weekly, and today they make up the 57 volumes of *The Metropolitan Tabernacle Pulpit.* He founded a pastor's college and several orphanages.

This sermon is taken from *The Metropolitan Tabernacle Pulpit,* volume 25, and was preached on July 20, 1879.

Charles Haddon Spurgeon

1

OUR MOTTO

With good will doing service, as to the Lord, and not to men (Ephesians 6:7).

THIS SENTENCE WAS expressly addressed to "servants," which term includes, and first of all intends, those who unhappily were slaves. There were many slaves in the Roman Empire, and the form of bondage that then existed was of the bitterest kind.

I can imagine a slave becoming a Christian and so finding peace as to his former guilt, and obtaining renewal of heart. Then, although rejoicing in the Lord, I can well conceive that he would often be downcast in view of his sad condition as a bondsman. I see him sitting down and moaning to himself: "I am a bondsman under a tyrant master. I have already endured many cruelties, and may expect many more. I would be free, but there is no hope of escape, since there is no place to which I can flee, for Caesar's arm is long. It would reach me at the very ends of the earth. I cannot purchase my liberty, nor earn it by long years of faithful servitude; neither can my fellow-bondsman effect our deliverance by rebellion, for this has been tried and has ended in terrible bloodshed. I am hopelessly a slave. What shall I do? How shall I sustain my fate? My life is well-nigh intolerable: would to God it were at an end."

I can imagine the poor bondsman going to his cramped up bed under the stair—for in any hole or corner the Roman slave might find such little rest as was allowed him—and there he would almost wish to sleep himself into another world. Being a Christian, as I have supposed, he pours out his heart before God in prayer, and in answer to his cry the Lord Jesus sets before him the rich consolation that he has provided for all that mourn—consolation strong enough to enable him to endure to the end, and glorify the name of Jesus even under such hard conditions.

While yet troubled in mind, this freeman of the Lord, who is yet in bonds to man, is met by the Savior himself. He appears to him—I will not say in such form as could be perceived by the eyes, but in vision clear enough to be exceedingly influential over his spirit. Jesus stands before him. The five wounds adorning him like precious rubies are infallible tokens; the face lit up with an unearthly splendor is still marked with the old lines of sorrow, and the head bears the thorn-crown still about its brow. The poor slave casts himself at his Redeemer's feet with astonishment, with awe, and with intense delight. Then I think I hear those dear lips, which are as lilies dropping sweet-smelling myrrh, saying to his poor servant, "Fulfill thy service bravely. Do it unto me. Forget thy tyrant master and remember only me. Bear on, work on, suffer on, and do all as unto me, and not unto men." Then I think I see the broken-hearted captive rising up refreshed with inward strength, and I hear him say, "I will even bear the yoke until my Lord shall call me away. Unless His providence shall open for me a door of liberty I will patiently abide where I am and suffer all His will. Hopefully and joyfully serve because *He* bids me do it for his sake."

The Motto: I serve

A vision that would so greatly comfort the poor Roman slave in his extremity may well stand before each one of us. Let us each hear our Savior say, "Live unto Me, and do all for My sake." Our service is so much more pleasant and easy than that of slaves, let us perform it "with good will doing service, as unto the Lord, and not to men." Our princely motto is "I serve." Be this sentence emblazoned on our banner, and used as the battle-cry of life's campaign.

Notice well that *the Holy Spirit does not bid us leave our stations in order to serve the Lord.* He does not bid us forego the domestic relations that made us husbands or wives, parents or children, masters or servants. He does not suggest to us to put on a peculiar garb and seek the seclusion of a hermitage, or the retirement of monastic or conventual life. Nothing of the kind is hinted at, but He bids the servant continue in his or her service—"with good will doing service." Our great Captain would not have you hope to win the victory by leaving your post. He would have you abide in your trade, calling, or profession, and all the while serve the Lord in it, doing the will of God from the heart in common things.

This is the practical beauty of our holy faith, that when it casts the devil out of a man it sends him home to bless his friends by telling them how great things the Lord has done for him. Grace does not transplant the tree, but bids it overshadow the old house at home as before, and bring forth good fruit where it is. Grace does not make us unearthly, though it makes us unworldly. True religion distinguishes us from others, even as our Lord Jesus was separate from sinners, but it does not shut us up or hedge us round about as if we were too good or too tender for the rough usage of everyday life. It does not put us in the salt box and shut the lid down, but it casts us in among our fellow men for their good. Grace makes us the servants of God while still we are the servants of men. It enables us to do the business of heaven while we are attending to the business of earth. And it sanctifies the common duties of life by showing us how to perform them in the light of heaven. The love of Christ makes the lowliest acts sublime. As the sunlight brightens a landscape and sheds beauty over the commonest scene, so does the presence of the Lord Jesus. The spirit of consecration renders the offices of domestic servitude as sublime as the worship which is presented upon the sea of glass before the eternal throne, by spirits to whom the courts of heaven are their familiar home.

Our Motto: "As to the Lord, and not to men"

I suggest my text to all believers as the motto of

their lives. Whether we are servants or masters, whether we are poor or rich, let us take this as our watchword, *"As to the Lord, and not to men."* Henceforth may this be the engraving of our seal and the motto of our coat of arms; the constant rule of our life, and the sum of our motive. In advocating this gracious aim of our being, let me say that if we are enabled to adopt this motto it will, first of all, *influence our work itself:* and, secondly, it will *elevate our spirit concerning that work.* Yet let me add, thirdly, that if the Lord shall really be the all in all of our lives, *it is after all only what He has a right to expect,* and what we are under a thousand obligations to give to Him.

This Motto Will Influence Our Work

Our subject opens with this reflection, that if henceforth whether we live we live unto the Lord, or whether we die we die unto the Lord (Romans 14:8), *this consecration will greatly influence our entire work.* Do you say, my brother, that henceforth your whole life shall be a service of the Lord?

Then it will follow, *first, that you will have to live with a single eye to His glory.* See how in verse 5 we are told, "Servants, be obedient to them that are your masters according to the flesh, with fear and trembling in singleness of your heart, as unto Christ." If we do indeed live "as to the Lord," we must needs live wholly to the Lord. The Lord Jesus is a most engrossing Master. He has said, "No man can serve two masters" (Matthew 6:24) and we shall find it so. He will have everything or nothing. If indeed He be our Lord, he must be sole sovereign, for He will not tolerate a rival.

It comes to pass then, O Christian, that you are bound to live for Jesus and for Him alone. You must have no co-ordinate or even secondary object or divided aim. If you do divide your heart, your life will be a failure. As no dog can follow two hares at one time, or he will lose both, certainly no man can follow two contrary objects and hope to secure either of them. No, it behooves a servant of Christ to be a concentrated man. His affections should be bound up into one affection, and that affection should not be set on things on the earth, but on things above; his heart must not be divided, or it will be said of him as of those in Hosea, "Their heart is divided; now shall they be found wanting" (10:2).

The chamber of the heart is far too narrow to accommodate the King of kings and the world, or the flesh, or the devil, at the same time. We have no wish, desire, ambition, or exertion to spare for a rival lord. The service of Jesus demands and deserves all. Such is the eminence of this object, that all a man has or can have of reason or strength must be spent this way if he is to win. Nor is this too much for our great Lord to expect from those for whom he has done so much. To whom should I give a part of myself, my Master? Thou hast redeemed me wholly, and I am altogether thine, take thou full possession of me! Who else can be worthy of my heart? Who else can have a right to set foot within the province whereof Thou art the King? Nay, rule alone, Thou blessed and only Potentate! As Thou alone hast redeemed me, treading the winepress of wrath alone for me, so shalt Thou be sole monarch of my soul! Thou art all my salvation and all my desire, and therefore thou shall have all my homage and service. With such a Lord to be served, the current of our life must run in one sole channel, that He may have it all and none may run to waste.

Next, *to do service to the Lord we must live with holy carefulness,* for what said the context? We are to serve "with fear and trembling" (v. 5). In the service of God we should use great care to accomplish our very best, and we should feel a deep anxiety to please Him in all things.

There is a trade called paper-staining, in which a man flings colors upon the paper to make common wall decorations, and by rapid processes acres of paper can be speedily finished. Suppose that the paper-stainer should laugh at an eminent artist because he had covered such a little space, having been stippling and shading a little tiny piece of his picture by the hour together, such ridicule would itself be ridiculous. Now the world's way of religion is the paper-stainer's way, the daubing way. There is plenty of it, and it is quickly done. But God's way, the narrow way, is a careful matter; there is but little of it, and it costs thought, effort, watchfulness, and care. Yet see how precious is the work of art when it is done and how long it lasts, and you will not wonder that a man spends his time upon it: even so true godliness is acceptable with God, and it endures for ever, and therefore it well repays the earnest effort of the man of God. The miniature painter has to be very careful of every touch and tint, for a very little may spoil his work. Let our life be a miniature painting; "with fear and trembling" let it be wrought out.

We are serving the thrice Holy God, who will be revered by all that come near to him, let us mind what we do. Our blessed Master never made a faulty stroke when he was serving his Father; he never lived a careless hour, nor let drop an idle word. Oh, it was a careful life he lived. Even the night watches were not without the deep anxieties that poured themselves forth in prayer unto God: and if you and I think that the first thing which comes to hand will do to serve our God with, we made a great mistake, and grossly insult His name. We must have a very low idea of His infinite majesty if we think that we can honor Him by doing his service half-heartedly, or in a slovenly style. No, if you will indeed live "as to the Lord, and not unto man," you must watch each motion of your heart and life, or you will fail in your design.

Living as to the Lord means living with a concentrated spirit and living with earnest care that our one service may be the best of which we are capable when at our best estate. Alas, how poor is that best when we reach it! Truly, when we have done all, we are unprofitable servants, but that is seldom reached.

Further, if henceforth our desire is to live "as to the

Lord, and not unto men," *then what we do must be done with the heart.* "In singleness of your heart," says the context; and again in the sixth verse, "As the servants of Christ, doing the will of God from the heart." Our work for Jesus must be the outgrowth of the soil of the heart. Our service must not be performed as a matter of routine: there must be vigor, power, freshness, reality, eagerness, and warmth about it, or it will be good for nothing. No fish ever came upon God's altar because it could not come there alive; the Lord wants none of your dead, heartless worship. You know what is meant by putting heart into all that we do; explain it by your lives. A work that is to be accepted of the Lord must be heart-work throughout—not a few thoughts of Christ occasionally, and a few chill words and a few change gifts, and a little done by way of by-play—but as the heart beats so must we serve God: it must be our very life. We are not to treat our religion as though it were a sort of off-hand farm that we were willing to keep going but not to make much of, our chief thoughts being engrossed with the home farm of self and the world, with its gains and pleasures. Our Lord will be *aut Caesar aut nullus,* either ruler or nothing. My Master is a jealous husband: He will not tolerate a stray thought of love elsewhere, and He thinks it scorn that they who call themselves His beloved should love others better than himself. Such unchastity of heart can never be permitted, let us not dream of it.

We may not claim to be His if we give Him only lip service, and brain service, and hand service; He must have the heart. *Oh, our beloved Lord, You did not spare Your heart from agony for us. The lance set it abroach with all its costly double flood for our unworthy sakes; therefore You cannot be content to receive in return lifeless forms and cold pretences. You did live indeed; there was no sham about thy life. In all you did, You were intense. The zeal of your Father's house had eaten you up. You were clad with zeal as with a cloak with covered Thee from head to foot. Let us live somewhat after this glorious fashion, for your servant only truly lives when he lives as his Master.* "He that is perfect shall be as his Master" (Luke 6:40).

If we are to live to the Lord, the fountains of our soul must flow with boiling floods, and our life must be like a great Icelandic geyser casting us its columns of water, which seethe and boil as they rise. As great earthquakes shake the very center, so must there be movements of life within us which stir our soul with vehement longings for Jesus and with intense yearnings for his glory. All our light and life must turn to love, and that love must be all on flame for Jesus. If we truly live unto Christ, it must be so.

What else said the passage before us? If we say, henceforth I will do the will of God as to the Lord and not unto men, *then we must do it under subjection:* for note well the words, "doing the will of God." Some people's religion is only another way of doing their own will. They pick and choose what precepts they shall keep and what they shall neglect, what doctrines they shall hold and what they shall refuse: their spirit is not bowed into sacred servitude, but takes license to act according to its own pleasure. The freedom of a Christian lies in what I will venture to call an absolute slavery to Christ; and we never become truly free till every thought is brought into subjection to the will of the Most High.

Now if henceforth I live to God, I have no longer any right to say, "I will do this or that," but I must inquire, "My Master, what would thou have me to do?" As the eyes of the maidens are to their mistress, so are our eyes up to thee, O Lord. Believer, thy Master is to will for thee henceforth. It is idle to say, "I shall live as to the Lord and not unto men," when all the while we intend to live in our own fashion. Which is to be master now, self or Christ? On every point this question must be settled: for if on any point we assume the personal mastery the rule of Jesus is wholly refused. To go or to stand still, to suffer or to be in pleasure, to be in honor or to be in disgrace, is no more to be at our option. If we have a momentary choice, it is to be cheerfully resigned before the sovereignty of Him whom we have now taken to be our all in all. There is no being a Christian if Christ does not have the throne in the heart and life. It is but the mockery of Christianity to call Jesus Master and Lord while we do not the things which he commands.

We must do all this under a sense of the Divine oversight. Notice in verse 6 it is said of servants, "Not with eyeservice, as men-pleasers." What a mean and beggarly thing it is for a man only to do his work well when he is watched. Such oversight is for boys at school and mere hirelings. You never think of watching noble-spirited men. Here is a young apprentice set to copy a picture: his master stands over him and looks over each line, for the young scapegrace will grow careless and spoil his work, or take to his games if he be not well looked after. Did anybody thus dream of supervising Raphael and Michaelangelo to keep them to their work? No, the master artist requires no eye to urge him on. Popes and emperors came to visit the great painters in their studios, but did they paint the better because these grandees gazed upon them? Certainly not; perhaps they did all the worse in the excitement or the worry of the visit. They had regard to something better than the eye of pompous personages. Likewise, the true Christian wants no eye of man to watch him. There may be pastors and preachers who are the better for being looked after by bishops and presbyters; but fancy a bishop overseeing the work of Martin Luther, and trying to quicken his zeal; or imagine a presbyter looking after Calvin to keep him sound in the faith. Oh, no; gracious minds outgrow the governance·and stimulus that come of the oversight of mortal man.

God's own Spirit dwells within us, and we serve the Lord from an inward principle, which is not fed from without. There is about a real Christian a prevailing sense that God sees him, and he does not care who else may set his eye upon him; it is enough for him that

God is there. He hath small respect to the eye of man, he neither courts nor dreads it. Let the good deed remain in the dark, for God sees it there, and that is enough; or let it be blazoned in the light of day to be pecked at by the censorious, for it little matters who censures since God approves. This is to be a true servant of Christ: to escape from being an eye-servant to men by becoming in the sublimest sense an eye-servant, working ever beneath the eye of God. If we did but realize this, how well we should live! If now I recollect, as I try to do, that God hears each word I speak to you from this pulpit; that he reads my soul as I address you in his name, how ought I to preach? And if you go to your Sunday school class this afternoon, and picture Jesus sitting among the boys and girls, and hearing how you teach them, how earnestly you will teach. At home when you are about to scold a servant; or in the shop, when you think to do a rather sharp thing, if you think your Master stands there and sees it all, what a power it will have over you! Our lives should all be spent under the spell of "Thou God seest me" (Genesis 16:13), and we should each be able to declare, "I have set the Lord always before me" (Psalm 16:8).

One more thought, and it is this. If henceforth we are to serve the Lord, and not men, *then we must look to the Lord for our reward, and not to men.* "Knowing," said the eighth verse, "that whatsoever good thing any man does, the same shall he receive of the Lord, whether he be bond or free." Wage! Is that the motive of a Christian? Yes, in the highest sense, for the greatest of the saints, such as Moses, have "had respect unto the recompense of the reward" (Hebrews 11:26), and it were like despising the reward that God promises to His people if we had no respect whatever unto it. Respect unto the reward that comes of God kills the selfishness that is always expecting a reward from men. We can postpone our reward, and we can be content instead of receiving present praise, to be misunderstood and misrepresented. We can postpone our reward, and we can endure instead thereof to be disappointed in our work, and to labor on without success, for when the reward does come how glorious it will be! An hour with Jesus will make up for a lifetime of persecution! One smile from Him will repay us a thousand times over for all disappointments and discouragements.

Thus you see, brethren, that if we do in very deed make this our rule and maxim—"As to the Lord, and not to men"—our work will be shaped and fashioned most wonderfully. May God grant that the influence of this motive may manifestly sway our whole life henceforth, until we close it for this world, and commence it anew where we shall no need to shift our course, but shall continue eternally to live to the Lord alone.

Our Motto Will Elevate Our Spirit

May the Holy Spirit guide us while we reflect, secondly, that should this text become the inspiration of our life *it would greatly elevate our spirits.* What would it do for us?

First, it would lift us above all complaining about the hardness of our lot, or the difficulty of our service. "Alas," says one, "I am worn out. I cannot keep on at this rate. My position is so terribly trying that I cannot hold on much longer: it strains not only muscle and sinew, but nerve and heart. Nobody could bear my burden long: my husband is cruel, my friend is unkind, my children are ungrateful." Ah, poor heart, there are many others who wear the weeping-willow as well as thyself. But be of good courage, and look at thy case in another light. If the burden is to be borne for Jesus' sake, who loved thee and gave Himself for thee, by whose precious blood thou art redeemed from the pains of hell, can thou not bear it? "That is quite another thing," say you. "I could not bear it for a sneering master. I could not bear it for a passionate, froward mistress, but I could do anything and I could bear anything for Jesus." This makes all the difference—

> "For Him I count as gain each loss,
> Disgrace for Him, renown;

Well may I glory in His cross,
While He prepares my crown!"

We are satisfied to bear any cross so long as it is *His*
cross. What wonders men can do when they are
influenced by enthusiastic love for a leader! Alexander's
troops marched thousands of miles on foot, and they
would have been utterly wearied had it not been for
their zeal for Alexander. He led them forth conquering
and to conquer. Alexander's presence was the life of
their valor, the glory of their strength. If there was a
very long day's march over burning sands, one thing
they knew—Alexander marched with them. If they were
thirsty, they knew that he thirsted too, for when one
brought a cup of water to the king, he put it aside,
thirsty as he was, and said, "Give it to the sick soldier."
Once it so happened that they were loaded with the
spoil which they had taken, and each man had become
rich with goodly garments and wedges of gold. Then
they began to travel very slowly with so much to carry,
and the king feared that he should not overtake his
foe. Having a large quantity of spoil that fell to his
own share, he burned it all before the eyes of his soldiers
and bade them do the like that they might pursue the
enemy and win even more. "Alexander's portion lies
beyond," cried he. Seeing the king's own spoils on fire,
his warriors were content to give up their gains also
and share with their king. He did himself what he
commanded others to do: in self-denial and hardship
he was a full partaker with his followers.

After this fashion our Lord and Master acts towards
us. He says, in effect, "Renounce pleasure for the good
of others. Deny yourself, and take up your cross. Suffer,
though you might avoid it; labor, though you might
rest, when God's glory demands suffering or labor of
you. Have not I set you an example?" "Who, though he
was rich, yet for our sakes he became poor, that we
through his poverty might be rich" (2 Corinthians 8:9).
He stripped Himself of all things that He might clothe
us with His glory. O, brothers and sisters, when we
heartily serve such a leader as this, and are fired by

His Spirit, then murmuring, and complaining, and weariness, and fainting of heart are altogether fled: a divine passion carries us beyond ourselves.

> "I can do all things, or can bear
> All suffering if my Lord be there."

Next, this lifts the Christian above the spirit of stinting. I believe great numbers of working men—I am not going to judge them for it—always consider how little they can possibly do to earn their wages, and the question with them is not, "How much can we give for the wages?" that used to be; but, "How little can we give? How little work can we do in the day without being discharged for idleness?" Many men say, "We must not do all the work today, for we shall need something to do tomorrow: our masters will not give us more than they can help, and therefore we will not give them more than we are obliged to." This is the general spirit on both sides, and as a nation we are going to the dogs because that spirit is among us. We shall be more and more beaten by foreign competition if this spirit is cultivated.

Among Christians such a notion cannot be tolerated in the service of our Lord Jesus. It never does for a minister to say, "If I preach three times a week it is quite as much as anybody will expect of me; therefore I shall do no more." It will never be right for you to say, "I am a Sunday school teacher. If I get into the class to the minute—some of you do not do that—and if I stop just as long as the class lasts, I need not look after the boys and girls through the week. I cannot be bothered with them. I will do just as much as I am bound to do, but no more."

In a certain country town it was reported that the grocer's wife cut a plum in two, for fear there should be a grain more than weight in the parcel, and the folks called her Mrs. Split-plum. Ah, there are many Split-plums in religion. They do not want to do more for Jesus than may be absolutely necessary. They would like to give good weight, but they would be sorry to be convicted of doing too much. Ah, when we get to feel we are doing service for our Lord Jesus Christ, we adopt a far more liberal scale. Then we do not calculate how much ointment will suffice for His feet, but we give Him all that our box contains. Is this your talk, "Here, bring the scales, this ointment cost a great deal of money, we must be economical. Watch every drachm, yea, every scruple and grain, for the nard is costly"? If this be your cool manner of calculation, your offering is not worth a fig.

This was not the attitude of that daughter of love of whom we read in the gospels, she broke the box and poured out all the contents upon her Lord. "To what purpose is this waste?" (Matthew 26:8), cried Judas. It was Judas who thus spoke, and you know therefore the worth of the observation. Christ's servants delight to give so much as to be thought wasteful, for they feel that when they have in the judgment of others done extravagantly for Christ, they have but begun to show their hearts' love for His dear name. Thus the elevating power of the spirit of consecration lifts us up above the wretched parsimony of mere formality.

Again, this raises us up above all boasting of our work. "Is the work good enough?" said one to his servant. The man replied, "Sir, it is good enough for the price: and it is good enough for the man who is going to have it." Just so, and when we "serve" men we may perhaps rightly judge in that fashion, but when we come to serve Christ, is anything good enough for Him? Could our zeal know no respite, could our prayers know no pause, could our efforts know no relaxation, could we give all we have of time, wealth, talent, and opportunity, could we die a martyr's death a thousand times, would not He, the Best Beloved of our souls, deserve far more? Ah, that He would. Therefore is self-congratulation banished for ever. When you have done all, you will feel that it is not worthy of the matchless merit of Jesus, and you will be humbled at the thought. Thus, while doing all for Jesus stimulates zeal, it fosters humility, a happy blending of useful effects.

The resolve to do all as unto the Lord will elevate you

*above that craving for recognition which is a disease
with many.* It is a sad fault in many Christians that
they cannot do anything unless all the world is told of
it. The hen in the farmyard has laid an egg, and she
feels so proud of the achievement that she must cackle
about it: everybody must know of that one poor egg till
all the country round resounds with the news. It is so
with some professors: their work must be published, or
they can do no more. "Here have I," said one, "been
teaching in the school for years, and nobody ever
thanked me for it; I believe that some of us who do the
most are the least noticed, and what a shame it is."
But if you have done your service unto the Lord, you
should not talk so, or we shall suspect you of having
other aims. The servant of Jesus will say, "I do not
want human notice. I did it for the Master; He noticed
me, and I am content. I tried to please Him, and I did
please Him, and therefore I ask no more, for I have
gained my end. I seek no praise of men, for I fear lest
that breath of human praise should tarnish the pure
silver of my service."

*This would lift you above the discouragement which
sometimes comes of human censure.* If you seek the
praise of men, you will in all probability fail in the
present, and certainly you will lose it in the future
sooner or later. Many men are more ready to censure
than to commend; to hope for their praise is to seek for
sugar in a root of wormwood. Man's way of judging is
unjust, and seems fashioned on purpose to blame all of
us one way or another. Here is a brother who sings
bass, and the critics say, "Oh yes, a very fine bass
voice, but he could not sing treble." Here is another
who excels in treble, and they say, "Yes, yes, but we
prefer a tenor." When they find a tenor, they blame
him because he cannot take the bass. No one can be
candidly praised, but all must be savagely censured.
What will the great Master say about it? Will He not
judge thus—"I have given this man a bass voice, and
he sings bass, and that is what I meant him to do: I
gave that man a tenor voice, and he sings tenor, and

this is what I meant him to do: I gave that man a treble voice, and he sings treble, and so takes the part I meant him to take. All the parts blended together make up sweet music for my ears"?

Wisdom is justified of her children, but folly blames them all round. How little we ought to care about the opinions and criticisms of our fellowmen when we recollect that He who made us what we are and helps us by his grace to act our part, will not judge us after the mode in which men carp or flatter. He will accept us according to the sincerity of our hearts. If we feel, "I was not working for you; I was working for God," we shall not be much wounded by our neighbor's remarks. The nightingale charms the ear of night. A fool passes by and declares that he hates such distracting noises. The nightingale sings on, for it never entered the little minstrel's head or heart that it was singing for critics. It sings because He who created it gave it this sweet faculty. So may we reply to those who condemn us, "We live not unto you, O men: we live unto our Lord." Thus do we escape the discouragements that come of ungenerous misapprehension and jealous censure.

This, too, will elevate you above the disappointments of non-success—yes, even of the saddest kind. If those you seek to bless be not saved, you have not altogether failed. You did not teach or preach having the winning of souls as the absolute ultimatum of your work. You did it with the view of pleasing Jesus, and He is pleased with faithfulness even where it is not accompanied with success. Sincere obedience is His delight even if it lead to no apparent result. If the Lord should set His servant to plough the sea or sow the sand, he would accept his service. If we should have to witness for Christ's name to stocks and stones, and our hearers should be even worse than blocks of marble, and should turn again and rend us, we may still be filled with contentment, for we shall have done our Lord's will, and what more do we want? To plod on under apparent failure is one of the most acceptable of all works of faith, and he who can do it year after year is assuredly well-pleasing unto God.

This lifts us above disappointment in the prospect of death. We shall have to go away from our work soon, so men tell us, and we are apt to fret about it. The truth is that we shall go on with our work forever if our service is pleasing to the Lord. We shall please Him up yonder even better than we do here. And what if our enterprise here should seem to end as far as man is concerned. We have done it unto the Lord, and our record is on high, therefore it is not lost. Nothing that is done for Jesus will be destroyed. The flower may fade, but its essence remains. The tree may fall, but its fruit is stored. The cluster may be crushed, but the wine is preserved. The work and its place may pass away, but the glory which it brought to Jesus shines as the stars for ever and ever.

This lifts us above the deadening influence of age and the infirmities that come with multiplied years. What little we can do we do it all the more thoroughly for Jesus as our experience ripens. If we must contract the sphere, we condense and intensify the motive. If we are living unto Christ, we love Him even when our heart grows cold to other things. When the eye grows dim earthwards, it brightens toward heaven; when the ear can hardly hear the voice of singing men and singing women, it knows the music of Jesus' name; and when the hand can do little in human business, it begins feeling for the strings of its celestial harp that it may make melody for the Well-beloved. I know of nothing that can possibly elevate our spirit as workers for Christ like the sense of doing all unto the Lord and not unto men. May the Spirit of God help us to rise into this perfect consecration.

I have not time to say more than just this word. A due sense of serving the Lord would ennoble all our service beyond conception. Think of working *for Him,* for Him, the best of masters, before whom angels count it glory to bow. Work done for Him is in itself the best work that can be, for all that pleases Him must be pure and lovely, honest, and of good report. Work for the eternal Father and work for Jesus are works that are good and only good. To live for Jesus is to be swayed by the noblest of motives. To live for the incarnate God is to blend the love of God and the love of men in one passion. To live for the ever-living Christ is elevating to the soul, for its results will be most enduring. When all other work is dissolved, this shall abide. Men spoke of painting for eternity, but we in very deed serve for eternity.

Soon shall all worlds behold the nobility of the service of Christ, for it will bring with it the most blessed of all rewards. When men look back on what they have done for their fellows, how small is the recompense of a patriotic life! The world soon forgets its benefactors. Many and many a man has been born aloft in youth amidst the applause of men, and then in his old age he has been left to starve into his grave. He who scattered gold at first, begs pence at last: the world called him generous while he had something to give, and when he had bestowed all it this world blamed his imprudence. He who lives for Jesus will never have ground of complaint concerning his Lord, for He forsakes not His saints. Never man regretted anything he did for Jesus yet, save that he may regret that he has not done then times more. The Lord will not leave his old servants. "O God, thou has taught me from my youth: and hitherto have I declared thy wondrous works; now also when I am old and grey-headed, O God, forsake me not" (Psalm 71:17, 18), such was the prayer of David, and he was confident of being heard. Such may be the confidence of every servant of Christ. He may go down to his grave untroubled; he may rise and enter the dread solemnities of the eternal world without a fear, for service for Christ creates heroes to whom fear is unknown.

Our Motto Helps Us Do What God Deserves

I close by saying, that if we enter into the very spirit of this discourse, or even go beyond it—if henceforth we live for Jesus only, so as never to know pleasure apart from Him, nor to have treasure out of Him, nor honor but in His honor, nor success save in the progress of His kingdom, *we shall even then have done no more than He deserves at our hands.* First, we are God's *creatures.* For whom should a creature live but for his Creator? Second, we are His *new creatures* twice-born of heaven; should we not live for Him by whom we have been begotten for glory? As many as have believed in Jesus are the produce of that divine power which raised the Son of God from the dead, shall they not live in newness of life? God has taken this pains with us, that He has made us twice over, and He has made a new heaven and a new earth for us to dwell in; whom should we serve with all our mind but Him by whom we have been made anew? Third, we are *redeemed.* We are not our own, for we are bought with a price. We dare not be selfish: we may not put self in opposition to God, but I must go further—we may not allow self to be at all considered apart from God. Even when it seems that self and God might both be served at the same time, it must not be; self in any degree will spoil all. We are never to be masters, but servants always; and to serve ourselves is to make ourselves masters. Turn thine eyes, O my heart, to the cross and see Him bleeding there whom heaven adored: He is the light of glory, the joy and bliss of perfect spirits, and yet He dies there in pangs unutterable—dieth for me. O bleeding heart, my name was engraven upon thee! O tortured brain, thy thoughts were all of me! O Christ, Thou lovedst me and lovest me still, and that I should serve Thee seems but natural; that I should pray to serve with intense white-hot enthusiasm is an impulse of my life. Do you not confess it so, my brethren?

Besides, remember you are *one with Christ.* Whom should the spouse serve but her husband? Whom should the hand serve but the head? It scarce is service. Christ is your *alter ego,* your other self—no, your very self; should you not live for Him? You are bone of His bone and flesh of His flesh and therefore you must love Him. Let a divine selfishness impel you to love your Lord.

No hand, counts it hard to be serving his own head. Sure, it can be no hardness to do service to Him with whom we are joined by bonds and bands of vital union. He is our head, and we are His body and His fullness. Let us fill up His glory; let us spread abroad the praises of His name. God help us to finish this sermon never, but to begin it now and go on preaching it in our lives world without end. For heaven shall lie in this: "Not unto us, not unto us, but to Thy name be praise" and the beginnings of heaven are with us now, the youth, the dawn of glory, in proportion while we say from our very souls, "Whether we live, we live unto the Lord; and whether we die, we die unto the Lord; whether we live therefore, or die, we are the Lord's" (Romans 14:8). And so shall it be henceforth and for ever.

As to those that know nothing of this, because they know not Christ may the Lord bring them to believe in Jesus Christ this day, that they may through His grace become His servants. Amen and amen.

NOTES

Be Strong — and Work!

George Campbell Morgan (1863-1945) was the son of a British Baptist preacher and preached his first sermon when he was 13 years old. He had no formal training for the ministry, but his tireless devotion to the study of the Bible helped him to become one of the leading Bible teachers of his day. Rejected by the Methodists, he was ordained into the Congregational ministry. He was associated with Dwight L. Moody in the Northfield Bible conferences and as an itinerant Bible teacher. He is best known as the pastor of Westminister Chapel, London (1904-17 and 1933-35). During his second term there, he had Dr. D. Martyn Lloyd-Jones as his associate.

Morgan published more than 60 books and booklets, and his sermons are found in *The Westminister Pulpit* (London, Pickering and Inglis). This sermon is from Volume 8.

G. Campbell Morgan

2

BE STRONG — AND WORK!

Be strong . . . saith the Lord . . . and work: for I am with
you, saith the Lord of hosts (Haggai 2:4).

THESE WORDS WERE uttered about 2,500 years ago, yet
they come to us and to our day with a pertinence that
is almost startling. This is not surprising, for our times
have much in common with those of the old Hebrew
prophets. There are certain senses—the statement must
be made and received guardedly—in which the
prophetic writings made a profounder appeal to us than
do the apostolic writings. Men today *know* so much
more than they *do,* with the result that they begin to
question the things they know. That was the condition
in the time of the prophets. Therefore these prophetic
writings are powerful in the conditions addressed, in
the principles recognized, and in the appeals made. So
from this ancient writing of Haggai we take out these
words and find that they are living and powerful words,
coming to us not faint and far from that Eastern land
and that bygone time, but with an immediateness that
leads us to feel that they are verily the word of the
Lord to us.

In the book of Ezra we have the account of the laying
of the stones of the second temple.

Because a decree forbidding the work had been
obtained from Artaxerxes, the house of God lay waste
for fifteen years. It had that almost appalling aspect of
desolation, not of a structure battered and bruised and
beaten, and in some senses made beautiful by the
tempests and time, but of a structure commenced and
never finished. At the death of the king this edict lost
its authority, but the people did not proceed with the
building, citing difficulty, danger, and poverty as
reasons. Yet all the while neither danger nor difficulty

nor poverty prevented them from building their own houses—houses of beauty and luxury. To such a people the messages of Haggai came, and this brief prophecy of only two chapters tells the story of how he delivered these four prophecies in conjunction with Zechariah, and how the people arose and built the house of the Lord.

In our text three things are found with which I propose to deal: first, the need revealed by the command to "work"; second, the responsibility that rested on the people in view of the need; finally, the encouragement given to them to take up that responsibility and meet that need. The need was to build the house of God. The responsibility was that they should be strong and work. The encouragement was the promise and covenant that God made with them: "I am with you, said the Lord of hosts."

The Need for a House of God

The house of God has been neglected. We can imagine men saying: Why build this house? Why not wait? Why not leave the building to our children? The question was answered by the prophesyings of Haggai and Zechariah. One supreme answer was given to all such inquiry. It was the answer of the final, fundamental fact of all human life, the fact of God.

In one of his sermons at our Mundesley Bible Conference, my friend John A. Hutton said something which those of us who heard him will never forget, and he said it in such a way that we shall never forget. Speaking of the spies who went to spy out the land of Canaan and afterwards described themselves as grasshoppers, Mr. Hutton said that those men thought they were looking at the facts of the case, but they were not looking at facts, they were looking at circumstances. He declared that there is but one Fact, and that is God. All other things are circumstances related to that Fact. That is the underlying truth which made necessary the building of the house of God in that bygone age. God is the age-abiding Fact, the ever and everywhere present Fact, and men who forget Him are leaving out of their calculations the supreme quantity, and therefore their findings are inevitably doomed to be wrong.

A science that forgets God is blind, seeing only that which is near, and at last boasting itself that it has no interest in anything that is far. The philosophy that excludes God is equally incomplete, and therefore incompetent. Science starts with emptiness of mind and perfectly proper attitude. Philosophy starts with a question, What is truth? That is a perfectly fair method of operation. But science proceeding to the discovery of the facts will inevitably finally touch God. The question is whether it will dare to call Him God when it finds Him. That philosophy attempts to account for things and to give us the true wisdom of life must take God into account. The question is whether it will ultimately do so or not.

The one fact from which there is no escape is that fact of God. God is not distanced from human life. In Him we live and move and have our being (Acts 17:28). God is not uninterested in human life. If the great revelation of these sacred writings is to be trusted, there is absolutely nothing in which God is not interested.

In passing, let me urge very seriously those of you who have not been reading the Old Testament recently to read it once more, without prejudice, simply to see it as revealing God's interest in the common things of life, the commonplaces of life. It is the Old Testament that teaches you that God puts human tears into His bottle. It is the Old Testament that tells that God knows whether the garment you wear is a mixture of wool and something else or not. The Old Testament tells us that God is interested in the fringes that people wear on their garments. Trivial things, you say. That is our God! He is the God of the infinitely small as well as of the infinitely great, not alienated from any part of human life, knowing our downsitting and our uprising, our going out and our coming in; near to us in the casual as well as in the critical, numbering the hairs of our head. That is the supreme Fact of life, and the Fact from which there can be no escape.

> Whither shall I go from Thy Spirit?
> Or whither shall I flee from Thy presence?
> If I ascend up into heaven, Thou art there:
> If I make my bed in Sheol, behold, Thou art there.

What unutterable folly, then, on the part of humanity or of man if it or he leaves God out of calculation.

Because God is the final and fundamental Fact in human life, therefore He is the supreme obligation. To do His will is individual salvation, is social salvation, is national salvation. One human life perfectly poised toward God and adjusted toward His good and perfect and beneficent will is a human life realized, fulfilled, and progressively glorious. A society, which the church of God ought to be, discovering His will, walking in the way of it, obedient to the light that ever shines more and more unto the perfect day, is a society within the boundaries of which there is no lonely soul, for when one weeps, all weep; when one laughs, all laugh. A nation seeking righteousness rather than revenue, eager to glorify God rather than to maintain its face in the world, is a nation great, secure, impregnable, mighty with essential might.

The supreme obligation on human life is its relationship to God, therefore it is important to build His house. In the days in which Haggai exercised his ministry, the building of the house was entirely material. The house was the true rallying point for the people, the place of worship, the place where men gathering together did not seek the presence of God, but remembered His presence, recognized His power, reminded their own hearts anew of the abiding fact of His covenant with them and of His perpetual care of them. Moreover, in that ancient Hebrew economy, the house of God was essentially the house of prayer for all nations, as our Lord Himself did say in the days of His flesh, quoting from the ancient prophecies. Then how supremely important it was that the house should be built. There, for fifteen years, having been raised but a few feet in all probability from the ground, the first few courses laid, it had stood desolate, overgrown with verdure, moss-covered, a perpetual revelation of the fact that people who bore the name of God had largely forgotten Him. The supreme need in that hour was not the rearrangement of policy with surrounding nations, not the rediscovery of a lost art, not increase in commerce; the supreme necessity was that the house of God should be built, the sacramental symbol of the nation's relationship to Him.

Today the house of God is no longer material; it is living, it is spiritual, it is the church of God, the church of God which is the house of the living God. In this world of ours the church of God in the divine economy is an institute of praise and prayer and prophecy. An institute of praise, a living temple of living souls whose eyes are toward the light, whose faces are irradiated with joy, who are living in the midst of the sorrows and desolations of time as men and women who have found mastery over sorrow and desolation in their fellowship with the unseen and eternal.

That is true of the Catholic Church, the whole church, and in that function of the church all the things that divide us cease to be, and we realize that the building of the church of God is of supreme importance in order that there may be maintained in the midst of the sorrows and sins of humanity a living testimony to the gladness and holiness that are possible to men as they live in right relationship with God. Nothing, therefore, can be more important than this building of the church, the building of it stone upon stone, of living stones brought into touch with the Living Stone, whose preciousness is made over to them that they may share that preciousness and bear testimony in their glad, pure, consenting life to what the Kingdom of God really means in the world.

Whereas the house of God today is no longer material but spiritual, the material is still a very real symbol of the spiritual. When the church of God in any place in any locality is careless about the material place of assembly, the place of its worship and its work, it is a sign and evidence that its life is at a low ebb.

Let us not, however, lose sight of the larger matter, the necessity for the continuation of the building of the spiritual house of God. There is nothing this nation needs more than that the church of God itself should be more clearly seen. Therefore there is no work more important than that of the continuity of the building of that spiritual house which, in the life of the nation, is not to be dictated to by the nation, but to exercise its threefold function of praise, prayer, and prophecy, and so contribute to the true essential strength of the national life.

The First Responsibility: To Be Strong

These words spoken in the olden days by the prophet indicated not only the need, but the responsibility. The spiritual value of this old-time story is here most marked, most definite. These people were to "be strong"; that is the first thing. And they were to "work"; that was the second. These two things cannot be separated. There can be no work apart from strength; there can be no strength, such as the prophet referred to, which does not express itself in work. "Be strong . . . and work."

This charge to the people was a suggestion of their weakness, the weakness that had prevented, and still was preventing, them from building the house of God. We discover the elements of the weakness in the most simple way by looking at the prophecy.

In the first place *their weakness consisted in the fact that they were careless about this matter.* They said, "It is not the time for us to come, the time for the Lord's houses to be built" (Haggai 1:2). That is so startlingly modern that I hardly know what to say about it. It is not the time! The modern man will not speak so simply; the modern man will say that it is not the psychological moment. That means the same thing. Whenever, in the presence of super abounding need, man says, "It is not the psychological moment," know well that the cleverness of his argument is revelation of the carelessness of his heart. The time is not come; we are waiting for the time, for some moment electric with inspirational opportunity. People who wait for that moment never find it, and do not want to find it.

Another element of weakness to which the prophet drew attention is revealed in the question he asked: "Is it a time for you yourselves to dwell in your cieled houses, while this house lieth waste?" (Haggai 1:4). *The second element of weakness in the life of the people was luxury and comfort*; they were dwelling in their own paneled houses, perhaps even while discussing over and over in their social gatherings the neglected condition of the house of God. The set time had not come to build it; but the time had come to build their own houses, and to panel them with beauty.

There was yet another element of weakness. We discover it by another question: "Who is left among you that saw this house in its former glory? And how do ye see it now? Is it not in your eyes as nothing?" (Haggai 2:3). *The third element of weakness was contempt for that very house which lay unfinished, and contempt for any man who suggested that it ever could be restored to its ancient glory.* This contempt was born of a great past, of which the people were always talking, and in which they rejoiced, to the neglect of the present, with its terrific responsibility and its glorious opportunity. The collateral writings to this prophecy reveal some of the reasons for the contempt. The sacred fire was no longer burning, the shekinah glory was no longer manifested, the ark and the cherubim were no longer in their places, the urim and the thummim had been lost, and the spirit of prophecy was silent. All these things were absent. The people looked back to the days when these things were there in all their glory, and they held the present in supreme contempt, both as to its conditions and as to the idea that it was possible to restore the lost glory.

I say again, the picture is wonderfully modern. We still have the carelessness which says, The time has not come. It expresses itself often in prayer for revival. The revival is here, if we will but have it so, I pray you talk no more about the indifference of the nation; talk if you will of the indifference of the church to its own evangel, its own gospel, its own living powers. The set time has not come, so men still say.

Then there is the weakness resulting from comfort. The church of God today is suffering from material prosperity within her own borders. Things which our fathers spoke of as luxuries we speak of as necessities. For all spiritual service we are being rendered weak, anemic, enervated by the beautiful houses and the comforts of our lives. The old Spartan heroism of our fathers, the simpler life, and the great poverty, have largely passed away. It is not the time to build the house of God, but it is the time to build our own houses and dwell in them.

Another element of weakness present with us is our perpetual looking back and sighing for departed glories, for the voice of preachers of other days, for the prayer meetings that once were held, for all those peculiar manifestations of the presence of God in past days. The old men are sighing for these and looking with contempt on the present hour, disbelieving in the possibility of revival and the building of the house of God.

Said the prophet to these men, and now says the Word of our God to us, "Be strong" (2:4). If we would know what our strength is, we may know it by examining our weakness. Over against every element of weakness we are to place an element of strength. Over against carelessness what shall we put? Listen to the voice of the prophet. "Consider your ways. Ye have sown much, and bring in little; ye eat, but ye have not enough; ye drink, but ye are not filled with drink; ye clothe you, but there is none warm; and he that earneth wages earneth wages to put it into a bag with holes. Thus saith the Lord of hosts: Consider your ways" (1:5-7). *One of the first conditions of real strength will be obedience to that command, the consideration of our ways.* The people were living in great material prosperity. But look more carefully: "Ye have sown much, and bring in little." But they had brought in very much, they were wealthy! "Ye eat, but ye have not enough"; but they always had enough to eat! "Ye drink, but ye are not filled with drink." But they always had enough to drink! "Ye clothe you, but there is none warm." But they always had plenty of clothing! "He that earneth wages earneth wages to put it into a bag with holes." But they had not discovered the holes! Mark the satire of it all. The prophet was declaring that in spite of all their getting they lacked the supreme possession; in spite of all their eating, there was hunger never satisfied; in spite of all their drinking, there was thirst never quenched; in spite of all their clothing, there was chilliness of soul that found no warmth; in spite of all their earning, there was a lack which nothing out of the bag into which they put their wages could provide! How true it all is today! The consideration of our ways is, indeed, the first necessity if we would be strong.

The second element of strength under such conditions was consciousness of the weakness of the house of God in its ruin, its devastation, of the fact that it stood there unfinished. Twice over the prophet said with infinite pathos: "This house lieth waste" (1:4, 9). I wonder when the one hundred and second psalm was written. It seems to me it must have been at a time in connection with this exhortation, or else the prophet was remembering it:

> Thou shalt arise, and have mercy upon Zion;
> For it is time to have pity upon her, yea, the set time is come (Psalm 102:13).

How did the psalmist know the set time had come? what was the sign for the arrival of the set time?

> For thy servants take pleasure in her stones,
> And have pity upon her dust (v. 14).

In that hour, when these men really looked at the

ruins, and the ruins entered into their heart and created great contrition, the set time came; they were then beginning to feel the element of strength.

Yet one other element of strength is revealed in the story. It is confidence in the promise and power of God: "I will fill this house with glory, saith the Lord of hosts . . . The latter glory of this house shall be greater than the former, saith the Lord or hosts: and in this place will I give peace, saith the Lord of hosts" (2:7, 9). When they believed that, they arose and built.

The Second Responsibility: To Work

The second part of the responsibility is revealed in the words: "and work." Work was to be opposed to idleness. That needs no argument. Work was to take the place of theorizing. I think that needs, if not argument, at least careful consideration. Far be it from me to speak with disrespect of efforts that may be in themselves most sincere. Yet sometimes I am appalled at the time we waste in considering things and theorizing about things. We call conferences to consider the situation, attempting to express Christianity in terms suited to the modern mind indeed, as though the modern mind mattered. On the other hand, we meet to consider the difficulty of the situation.

"Work" is the word of the Lord to us. We cannot travel a hundred yards from this place without finding some opportunity, if our eyes are open, to build the house of God by the capture of a soul, by a kindness, by a word of love, by a ministry of immediate help. In the work of building the house of God nothing is mean; the whole glorifies every part. That least thing you are doing, apparently so unimportant, is of supreme importance when you place it in relationship to the whole.

The last note of the text from the ancient prophecy is one full of encouragement. The prophet not merely drew attention to the need, not merely called to strength and to work; but in the name of God spoke to them this word of God: "I am with you, saith the Lord of Hosts" (2:4). Therefore, the things missing were not significant. These things also might be restored, the very things over which men were lamenting.

All this is most immediate and pertinent. "I am with you, saith the Lord of Hosts" (2:4). There is no need for us to gather together and pray for the coming of the Holy Spirit. There is no need for us to cry in our agony, "Awake, awake, put on strength, O arm of the Lord" (Isaiah 51:9). They did that also in the days of Isaiah, and God answered them: "Awake, awake, put on thy strength, O Zion" (52:1). If I may reverently say so, it is as though God had said, Why do you call on Me to awake? I have never been asleep! It is you who are asleep. When today we gather together to pray to God to come among us, it seems to me He would say, I am with you, even though you are unmindful of Me; even though you are not responsive to Me, I am with you. If we can but come to a new realization of the living presence and know that we have not to ask or wait for His coming, but that He is here waiting for us, then we shall arise and build. It is not true to say we need more of the Holy Spirit, but it is true to say that the Holy Spirit needs more of us. In that realization of the nearness of our God we shall find strength for all He is calling us to do.

The prophet named God by one of the great titles of the Old Testament, "The Lord of hosts" (1:2). He is the Lord of all Hosts. He is the Lord of His people who are called to work; He is Lord of the enemies who would attempt to prevent them from working, making the wrath of men to praise Him. "If God be for us, who can be against us?" (Romans 8:31). He is the Lord, not merely of the hosts of the earth, but of the hosts of heaven also, the hosts of the spiritual world. He is Lord of all angels, all unfallen ones, and of the spirits of just men made perfect. Angels, and the spirits of the just made perfect under His dominion are filled with praise of Him and inspired by His love. In some strange mystery which we may not understand, they are cooperative with His purpose even now. How many of us need the vision that was given to the young man with Elisha of old? Said he, "Behold, an host with horses and chariots was round about the city. . . . Alas, my master! how shall we do?" And the prophet said, "Lord, I pray Thee, open his eyes, that he may see" (2 Kings 6:15). And the Lord opened the eyes of the young man, and he saw; and, behold, the mountain was full of horses and chariots of fire (v. 17).

> So to Faith's enlightened sight
> All the mountain flamed with light!

He is also the Lord of the fallen ones. When He was incarnate, how often they cried out to Him: "What is there between Thee and us, Thou Jesus of Nazareth? Art Thou come to destroy us? I know Thee Who Thou art, the Holy One of God" (Luke 4:34). Then came the answer of the One of supreme authority and almighty power: "Hold thy peace, and come out of him" (v. 35). All the spiritual forces of the spiritual world against us are held in check by the power of God; or to put it as I have so often put it here, for I love the truth, I joy in it: Satan cannot touch a single hair on the back of one of Job's camels until he has asked permission of God. If what the nation and the world supremely need is the building of the house of God, what the church supremely needs is a new vision of God, a new consciousness of His nearness.

> Hell is nigh, but God is nigher,
> Circling us with hosts of fire!

The Lord and Master said to His disciples before He left them, "Lo, I am with you always" (Matthew 28:20). In the lonely island washed by the waters of the sea John heard a voice, and the voice said: "I am the Alpha and the Omega, saith the Lord God, which is, and which was, and which is to come, the Almighty" (Revelation 1:8). Then he "turned to see the voice which spake" (v. 12), and this is what he saw: "I saw seven golden candlesticks; and in the midst of the candlesticks one like unto a son of man, clothed with a garment down to the foot, and girt about at the breast with a golden girdle. And his head and his hair were white as white wool, white as snow; and his eyes were as a flame of fire; and his feet like unto burnished brass, as if it had been refined in a furnace; and his voice as the voice of many waters" (vv. 12-15).

That was the last appearing of God to man, figurative, symbolic, suggestive, and that to help us to understand Him when He says, "I am with you all the days."

The command and the promise were alike enforced by the words, "Thus saith the Lord." "Be strong . . . saith the Lord . . . and work; for I am with you, saith the Lord of hosts." That is overwhelming in compulsion and confidence. The story has often been told of Livingstone. When all alone, hemmed in by hostile tribesmen, waiting apparently for death, he wrote:

> I read that Jesus said, "All power is given unto Me in heaven and earth. Go ye therefore, and teach all nations . . . and, lo, I am with you always, even unto the end of the world" (Matthew 28:19-20).

Then follow these significant words:

> It is the word of a gentlemen of most sacred and strictest honor, and there's an end on't. I will not cross furtively by night as I had intended. It would appear as flight, and shall such a man as I flee? Nay, verily I will take observations for latitude and longitude tonight, though they may be the last.

When the morrow came, he crossed without harm from the midst of hostile multitudes.

With all reverence, may we not say, as God says to us, "Be strong . . . and work; for I am with you"? "It is the word of a gentlemen of most sacred and strictest honor, and there's an end on't." So God help us:

> To the work! To the work! We are servants of God,
> Let us follow the path that our Master has trod;
> With the balm of His counsel our strength to renew,
> Let us do with our might what our hands find to do.

The Courage of Consecration

Hugh Black (1868-1953) was born and trained in Scotland and ministered with Alexander Whyte at Free St. George's in Edinburgh. He served as professor of Homiletics at Union Theological Seminary, New York (1906-1938), and was widely recognized as a capable preacher.

This sermon is taken from *Listening to God* by Hugh Black, published in 1906 by Fleming H. Revell Company, New York.

Hugh Black

3

THE COURAGE OF CONSECRATION

And I said, should such a man as I flee? (Nehemiah 6:11).

THE MEMOIRS OF Nehemiah present to us a record of noble endeavor, and show us what can be achieved by one man of courage and faith, whose life is ruled by unswerving allegiance to duty. They reveal Nehemiah as a man of deep feeling and tireless energy and stern resolution. He has his place in the history of revelation, not because of any profound thought on the problems of life, nor because of new insight into truth, but because of what he was enabled to do at a critical period of Israel's history. He was not a prophet who saw visions, nor a poet who interpreted the heart of man. He has no place in the long line of thinkers who have opened up new regions for the human spirit. He was rather a man of affairs, keen, practical, with genius for organization, a born leader of men, a man of iron nerve and passionate energy. He was the typical statesman in a day of small things, rather than the typical prophet like Isaiah, who was a statesman also, but with larger vision and dealing with wider interests. He was a practical businessman throwing his great capacities into a work for the good of his nation.

In a time like ours, when such qualities stand so high in public estimation, and among a people like us more noted for energy than for thought, for business than for vision, it is encouraging to note how similar capacities were in Nehemiah's case used for the kingdom of heaven. All the powers that dwell within a man can find ample scope, if they be only set to noble ends. Nothing is common and unclean among man's gifts if it be but consecrated. The church will not take her rightful place and perform her perfect work until she can command these qualities so common in our midst, until men realize that they are called to give of all they have to her service.

Enthusiasm for social progress, business talent, power of organization, capacity to deal with practical affairs, even financial genius, all those attributes most highly developed today, should be offered in greater degree than they are. Men who possess them are as much bound to devote them to larger ends than merely selfish ones, as men endowed with the rarer gifts of brain and heart.

This is surely one great lesson from the life of Nehemiah. If he had not consecrated these gifts, he would have been nothing but a successful man of affairs, or a high-placed permanent official, or a skillful counseler at the Persian court. Because in the power of a simple faith he gave himself to a great work, he stands in the succession of prophets and psalmists and saints and apostles, having spent himself for the kingdom of God. Can any personal success compare with taking a share in the coming of the kingdom? We need a higher conception of service, the consecration of all gifts to the service of God and men. Without this, it will be to find at the last that you have spent your strength for nothing and have given your labor for vanity.

Another lesson from Nehemiah's example is the lesson of courage that will not be daunted by difficulties, resolution to adhere to the path of duty, let come what may. The incident to which our text refers is an illustration of this. The task to which Nehemiah set himself was one, he soon discovered, which demanded all his energy and perseverance. Surrounded by the hostility of implacable foes of Jerusalem, who would stick at no treachery to prevent the fulfilment of his purposes, he had to fan the flickering flame of patriotism within his own countrymen. The enmity outside was no greater than the feebleness and cowardice within. A less stout-hearted man would have given up in despair, when he learned to what lengths of treachery his opponents were prepared to go. Cajolements, threats, charges of conspiracy against the King of Persia, open violence and covert attack, were all hurled at him, and all failed to make him even stop the work for a moment. He only said, "O God, strengthen my hands" (Nehemiah 6:9), as he drove on with his great task of building the walls of the city and securing it against attack.

Even the word of a prophet was perverted to force him to desist. Shemaiah pretended to reveal a plot formed against him, and as if in terror for him and for himself, besought him to take refuge in the temple. "Let us go together to the house of God within the temple; for they will come to slay thee; yea, in the night will they come to slay thee" (6:10). It was a mean plan to compass Nehemiah's ruin in another way—to make him ruin himself. It was the height of impiety for a man who was not a priest to trespass in the temple; and for the governor to do this to save his life would have alienated from him the sympathy of all the best people in the city, all the pious Jews who were his chief supporters. Shemaiah's veiled argument is that the safety of such an important life as that of the governor was of more value than the punctilious keeping of a temple law.

The force of the temptation to a religious man like Nehemiah was that the advice came to him through the mouth of a prophet. It seemed as if God commanded him to follow it. But he judged the counsel by his own moral sense and perceived that it was false; for God could not ask him at once to neglect his plain duty and at the same time commit a sin against the ceremonial law. He saw that the prophet was hired by his enemies to frighten him and compel him to do what would be accounted a sin, and thus have matter for an evil report to undermine his influence and achieve their own base designs. His answer was in keeping with his own resolute life. "Should such a man as I flee? Who is there that being such as I would go into the temple to save his life? I will not go in" (6:11). If need be he would die at his post. Not even to escape assassination could he, the leader of the great enterprise, show the white feather. The place of duty might be a place of danger, but he dare not flinch from it on that account. Humanly speaking, everything depended on him; and for him to weaken and desert even to save his life would be to ruin the cause. Instead of the fact of his being governor being an excuse for considering his own safety, it was the very opposite. Just because he was in a position of responsibility with every eye on him, and because there lay on him a heavy burden of duty, he must be true even though it should mean death. "Should such a man as I flee?" (6:11).

The courage that Nehemiah displayed was the courage of faith. He felt himself called to do this work, and he would do it at any cost. He believed that God was with him, and he was not going to turn tail and flee at the first sign of danger. There is a courage that is common enough, the courage of hot blood, which is a sort of animal instinct. It seems even constitutional in some races. This physical courage is only what we expect in men of our breed, an inheritance from our ancestors. We so seldom see past the surface that we often mistake the very qualities which compose the highest kind of courage. We praise a man because we say he does not know fear; but this may be mere insensibility. Some courage is due to want of thought, or want of imagination, or want of care for other. It may be only a dare-devil recklessness. But true courage needs to have something more in it than this quality of hot blood.

Alexander Dumas, in his great character of D'Artagnan, whom he meant to be the typical brave soldier, gives a touch which shows how real courage implies sensitive feeling mastered by a strong will. "D'Artagnan, thanks to his ever-active imagination, was afraid of a shadow; and ashamed of being afraid, he marched straight up to that shadow, and then became extravagant in his bravery if the danger proved to be real." Even physical courage is not simply absence of fear, not simply thoughtless, heedless daring. It needs to be related to a moral quality before it can take any high place as a virtue.

This true courage is rather steadfastness of mind, the calm, resolute fixity of purpose that holds to duty in the scorn of consequence. Nehemiah displayed this kind of courage when, alive to the presence of danger, knowing well the risk and counting all the cost, he turned upon the tempter with the indignant question, "Should such a man as I flee?" (6:11). He stood in the path of duty, and therefore in the very line of God's will, and he would not budge one inch. Martin Luther showed the same courage when the Elector wrote to him before the Diet of Worms reminding him that John Huss had been burnt at the Council of Constance, although he also possessed a safe-conduct. Luther replied that he would go to Worms if there were as many devils there as tiles on the roofs. He knew well that the chances were that he was going to his death; but he also knew that he was obeying conscience and obeying the truth by going. To his dear friend Melanchthon, who was in distress at their parting, he said, "My dear brother, if I do not come back, if my enemies put me to death, you will go on teaching and standing fast in the truth: if *you* live, *my* death will matter little." He too, like Nehemiah, was sustained by the thought of duty, by the sense of responsibility as the leader of a great movement, and by a resolute faith in God. "Should such a man as I flee?"

There is no quality more necessary for noble living than this moral courage; and there is no quality the lack of which is responsible for more failures. Courage of a sort is common enough, but this courage is rare, this steadfastness of heart, this unmovable adherence to duty, which turns an obstinate face to temptation, whether it come in the form of allurement or in the form of threat. Yet without it a strong character cannot possibly be formed. What examples we are of weakness of will, infirmity of purpose, instability of life, indecision of character. We need more iron in our blood. We need to have our natures hardened to withstand. Young men and young women need to think a little less of pleasure and a little more of duty. We give in to every dominant impulse though sheer moral cowardice and feebleness of mind.

In its essence, great courage like Nehemiah's is great faith. It was because he believed in God, and believed that he was doing God's will, that he was able to rise above all selfish fears. This is the secret of strength. As the psalmist said, "I have set the Lord always before me; because He is at my right hand, I shall not be moved" (Psalm 16:8). Well might Nehemiah be strong and of a good courage when he felt himself within the sweep of God's purpose, when he had emptied his heart of all selfish desires and sought only to do God's will. Well might he say, "Should such a man as I flee?" (6:11)—a man sure of himself because sure of God, a man privileged to undertake a great work, a man who feels himself a co-worker with God for the high ends of His Kingdom. It is only the same cause that can produce the same effect. If we had the same simple confidence in God, the same submission to His will, the same consecration of all our powers, we would have something of the same calm courage. If we made more of duty, and took the burden humbly on our shoulders, we would be strengthened by the very bearing of the burden to endure it. Faith is the true method of life, after all. Courage is the true way to high success. A sense of duty to God will save a man from weakness, will breed in him the iron nerve and steadfast courage and the endurance which is the crowning quality of great hearts.

> Not once or twice in our rough island story
> The path of duty was the way to glory.

And if the path of duty be not to all the way to glory in the large public sense in which Tennyson used these words about the Duke of Wellington, it will be at least the way to peace and true honor. Unless there be in a man's life a sense of duty that makes certain things necessary, things that he ought to do and must do, and certain things that he must refuse and will refuse at all costs, how can he escape being weak and wavering? He is the fit mark for any sudden and swift temptation. Unless a man can take his stand upon right and stiffen his neck against temptation to desert it, how can he expect to avoid open shame somewhere? Without it you are the victims—never the masters—of your fate. Till you have some courage of conviction, refusing to follow even a multitude to do evil, till you know the bit and the bridle and the spur of duty, going its way and not your own way, you are useless for the world's best ends. Till you have learned to say No, everlasting No, on some subjects; No, everlasting No, to some enticements, you have not begun to live as a moral being. There is nothing that our young men and women need more today than this courage, which adds a hard fiber to conscience, and gives stability to character. We are too pliant and flexible and flabby, too easily cowed into giving up principles, too easily moved by a sneer, too easily browbeaten by a majority, too timid in following our own best instincts. The sense of duty, paramount and supreme, seems weakened in our midst.

Duty cannot be maintained as an inviolate rule of life without moral courage; and courage cannot be maintained without consecration. Thus it is religion that preserves sacredness to human duty. It is the inspiring fount of noble endeavor. When a man is consumed with the desire to please God, he is long past the mere desire to please self. When the heart is fixed, the feet naturally take the path of God's commandments. The new affection moves the life to new obedience. The love of Christ drives out the lower loves and gives power in the hour of temptation. Should such a man as I, redeemed, sanctified, with the seal on my brow and the cross on my heart, flee from my corner of the battlefield?

A Full Man—Stephen

Clovis Gillham Chappell (1882-1972) was one of American Methodism's best-known and most effective preachers. He pastored churches in Washington, D.C.; Dallas and Houston, Texas; Memphis, Tennessee; and Birmingham, Alabama; and his pulpit ministry drew great crowds. He was especially known for his biographical sermons that made biblical characters live and speak to our modern day. He published about thirty volumes of sermons.

This message was taken from *More Sermons on Biblical Characters,* published in New York in 1930 by Richard R. Smith, Inc.

4

A FULL MAN—STEPHEN

And Stephen, full of faith and power, did great wonders
and miracles among the people (Acts 6:8).

DURING THE BUSY and eventful weeks immediately
following the Day of Pentecost, people separated by
wide chasms were brought into the fold of the Christian
brotherhood. Among this number were foreign-born
Jews and home-born Jews. These had hated each other
heartily in the past, but now they were being welded
together by the bonds of their common faith in Jesus
Christ. This growing spirit of brotherliness, however,
was not permitted to continue without hindrance.
Something took place at the time of our story that
came very near splitting the infant church into angry
and opposing factions.

The cause of this unfortunate situation was this:
many of the recent converts to Christianity were not
allowed to return home. They were cut off from all
financial support. They stood face to face with pinching
poverty. To meet the demand for immediate help, big-
hearted men came forward, such as Barnabas, who
gave their all to the support of these needy and
homeless converts. The funds thus obtained were put
into the hands of the apostles and were administered
by them.

But for some reason the administration of the Twelve
did not prove satisfactory. The foreign-born Jews
became convinced that they were not getting a square
deal. They claimed that their widows were neglected
in the daily ministration. Then the Apostles very wisely
decided to remedy the evil by a further organization of
the church. They saw that they themselves had been
undertaking too much. They realized that they had
been giving their time and their energies to a much

needed work, but to a work to which they were not especially and divinely called.

For this reason Peter and his fellow apostles came before the multitude with this wise suggestion: "It is not reason that we should leave the Word of God, and serve tables. Therefore, look ye out among you seven men full of the Holy Spirit and wisdom, whom we may appoint over this business. But we will give ourselves continually to prayer and to the ministry of the word" (Acts 6:2-4). That was an exceedingly wise decision. And great is the pity that all ministers of the gospel have not exercised the same high and holy wisdom.

That these apostles were in danger of being side-tracked. They were in danger of giving all their time to work to which they had not been appointed. Had they done so, they would have lost much of their effectiveness in their own divinely appointed work. And the danger that they faced and avoided is one that has only grown greater with the passing of the years. In our day, the machinery of the Church has been greatly multiplied. Preachers are better trained today then they have ever been before. But I am afraid that the modern church, with all its weak spots, is weakest in its pulpit. We as ministers have become skilled in many ways, but we have done so at a great price. Too often we have lost our skill at doing the supreme things. We have forgotten how to "give ourselves continually to prayer and the ministry of the Word" (Acts 6:4).

When the multitude heard the suggestion of Peter and his fellow apostles, they greeted it with hearty welcome. And it is my opinion that there was at least one name that was immediately suggested to almost every man and woman that was then present. "They are going to select seven men to administer the temporal affairs of the Church? Then I know one who is just exactly fitted to be president of that committee. I know one who is exactly the man to be Chairman of the Board." So one of the listeners said to his neighbor. And the neighbor answered immediately: "Yes, I thought of him the instant Brother Peter made the suggestion. You are thinking of our young brother, Stephen, no doubt." And so he was and so was almost everybody else. Thus Stephen was chosen and was made president. And I have a fancy that his election was unanimous.

Now it is with real pleasure that I introduce to you this morning Stephen, Chairman of the Board. This ancient lay preacher is one of the most charming personalities in all the history of the church. His whole story is told in two chapters of the New Testament. We watch him live for but one brief part of his life. We see him pass early and swiftly. But he abides long enough to leave his name written indelibly upon our minds and hearts. He appeals to us as embodying in himself the very highest and kingliest qualities of Christian manhood.

Dr. Luke's admiration for this gifted young man is very evident. He has one word that he applies to him again and again, and that is the word "full." In the estimation of Luke, there was fine well-roundedness, a fascinating fullness about Stephen. He did not impress Luke as being a fractional man. He was not a one-sided, half-baked individual. He was well-rounded, full-orbed. He was finely balanced, well grown. He impresses his biographer as one the elements of whose character were so mixed that nature might stand and say to all the world, "This is a man."

Stephen—full. But what is the next word? In what did Stephen's fullness consist? That is a supremely important question. There are some full folks that we cannot tolerate. We say, "I could like him, but he is so full of himself. He is so full of irony. He is so full of sarcasm. He is so full of trickery and treachery." There are some people who repel us because their souls are peopled with varied and unattractive demons.

Full of Faith

But what of Stephen? "Stephen, full of faith" (Acts 6:8). That is the first fine element of his fullness. He was a man not with a meager and timid and invalid faith. He was a man not with a sickly little handful of faith. He was a man full of faith, so full that though doubt came and knocked at his door every morning and every noon and every night, Stephen simply smiled and shook his head and said, "No room. Faith is my guest now." "Stephen, full of faith."

That means, of course, that Stephen was on good terms with God. That means that God delighted in Stephen and that Stephen delighted in God. That means that there was a fine intimacy between them, an intimacy that can exist in no other way. "For without faith it is impossible to please God. For he that cometh to God must believe that He is and that He is a rewarder of them that diligently seek Him" (Hebrews 11:6).

Not only was Stephen full of faith toward God, but he was also full of faith toward men. It does not take a wise man to see why this is true. How do we know that Stephen trusted people? How do we know that he believed in folks? Here is positive proof: folks believed in him. The whole brotherhood regarded him with fine firm trust and confidence. And cynics and misanthropes are never so trusted. If you put a question after everybody's name, do not forget that they will put that same kind of mark after yours. But faith begets faith.

Not only was Stephen full of faith, but he was full of wisdom. "The children of this world," said Jesus, "are wiser in their generation than the children of light" (Luke 6:8). Yes, that is true, but Stephen is a lovely exception. Stephen had a faith that could see visions and dreams, but he was more than a dreamer. He was a man of hard-headed common sense. He was a man who brought those faculties that would have made him a leader in the world of finance or of politics and dedicated them fully upon the altar of his Lord.

Full of Wisdom

"Stephen, full of wisdom." If there were hard

questions about the administration of the church, the people consulted Stephen. He was always ready with a suggestion that showed the keen insight of genius. If there was an individual with perplexities and problems with which he did not know how to cope, he came and talked with Brother Stephen about them. Though young in years he was wise. He was so wise that the keen historian Luke, writing under the inspiration of the Holy Spirit, said that he was "full of wisdom."

Full of Power

"Stephen, full of power." If there was a fine virtue that he seemed to be more full of than any other it is this of power. Where Stephen went, things happened. Changes took place, revolutions were wrought, and it stands written in the Record, "they were not able to resist the spirit and the wisdom by which he spake" (Acts 6:10). He was full of power. The word used for power here is the one from which we get our modern word, *dynamite*. This young saint was full of moral dynamite. He was a spiritual tornado. He swept things before him with an irresistible force.

Full of power—that is not the word that we may use about the church as a whole in this day of grace. Full of power—that is not the way we would go about describing most of the church members that we know. Full of power—that is not even the word that we would use to describe the majority of our ministers. Full of eloquence, it may be; full of learning; full of fine and gentlemanly qualities; full of a thousand desirable characteristics. But full of power—that is a description that, sad to say, describes only the few.

And yet was there ever a day when powerful saints were any more needed? Were they ever more needed in the pulpit and were they ever more needed in the pew? I know we have decency and respectability and kindness of heart. We have money and culture and social standing. But power—do we possess that absolute essential? "Mount Vernon Place Church, full of power."

Is that the way our church is entered upon the books of heaven? Is that a fit description of us as individuals? Surely it ought to be. Surely our oppositions are terrific enough to make power an absolute necessity. And yet we must realize that the term "full of weakness" would be a far better description of too many of us.

But, for our consolation and encouragement, let us bear in mind that this fine fullness may be ours. "Full of power" may as fitly describe you and me as it did Stephen of this far-off day. He who made men mighty centuries ago makes them mighty still wherever and whenever He has His way. "Ye shall receive power" (Acts 1:8), He is saying to us at this moment. "Tarry ye till ye be endued with power" (Luke 24:49). Oh, believe me, if our Christianity is the Christianity of the New Testament, it is a mighty something. It is a force in the presence of which the thunders of Niagara and the sweep of tornadoes will be as weak and trifling things.

Full of Grace

Then there is one more fullness that Luke ascribed to Stephen. "Stephen, full of grace." And when you hear that you recall that bejeweled sentence from John's Gospel: "And the Word became flesh and dwelt among us, . . . full of grace . . . " (1:14). Christ was full of grace. Christ's servant Stephen was also full of grace. That is, he was charming. He was magnetic. He was fascinating. He was attractive.

"Stephen, full of grace." He cast a spell over folks. He was as winsome as the springtime; as attractive as sea music. When folks were in his presence, they found themselves strangely comforted and helped. The broken-hearted forgot to sob when he was near. The hopeless forgot their despair. The wounded forgot their hurts. The barren and desert-hearted began to dream that the dreary wastes within their own souls might be made to rejoice and blossom as a rose. He was a gracious man.

And yet he did not win men merely to himself. What

says that bright star yonder that keeps eternal lids apart in the night sky? It says, "I owe my charm to another. I would have no beauty except it were given me. For me to shine is the sun." And so Stephen, full of grace, spoke to men of a gracious Savior. As they went away from listening to him they said, "I will go and learn something of his charm. I will go and consult the same Specialist that he has consulted, and see if He cannot smooth the care lines and the frown lines and the sin scars out of my own face."

"Stephen, full of grace." And that grace spoke in every tone of his voice. It looked out through his kindly eyes. It shone in every lineament of his face. "And they saw his face," the Record says, "as it had been the face of an angel" (Acts 6:15). Truly he had found the secret of real beauty. Ho, everyone who thirsts for real charm, everyone who longs to be genuinely and truly attractive, come and sit at the feet of the young preacher Stephen. He can show you how to become winsome with the very winsomeness of Jesus. He can show you how to lay hold on that which many of us lack so much and long for so much. He can show us how to be full of grace, full of charm, such grace and charm as cannot but be a blessing to the whole circle, whether large or small, that we are privileged to touch.

But you say, "That is well enough for Stephen living in the very shadow of Pentecost. But it is not possible for me. It is easy enough for Stephen to be full of these fine graces. But I have no hope personally of any such fullness. If I even made a start in that direction my life is soon depleted of its energies. All my moral forces are soon exhausted. Therefore, I see no hope for myself either for today or for tomorrow."

But before you reach this dismal conclusion, let us ask the secret of Stephen's fullness. What is the secret of the continued fullness of our old home spring down in Tennessee? It is not the fact that that spring never gives out any water. It is not the fact that no one ever stoops to drink its laughing life. It is giving, giving, giving all the time. Indeed it would exhaust itself in less than an hour but for one fact. It is fed from hidden and inexhaustible sources. Far back in the heart of the great hills is a reservoir that can give from generation to generation and never be exhausted.

And this is Stephen's secret. He is a greatly gifted young man. I am aware of that fact. There was not another man in the church in his day who had his ability. He had an intellect that in its wide and daring grasp of things was a rival to that of the apostle Paul. But this does not account for him. Neither is he accounted for by saying that he was a well-trained, a finely cultured young man.

What, then, is the secret? How comes he to be full of all the fine graces that we have mentioned? These are but the natural outcome of another fullness. It is mentioned by Luke in the very beginning and accounts for all else. Listen: "Stephen full of the Holy Spirit" (v. 5). Here then is the spring from which all these rivers flow. Here then is the sun that lighted all these winsome stars. You can only account for Stephen's graces and fine enviable qualities by saying that he was a man in whom Christ dwelt in the person of the Holy Spirit.

And surely this blessed fullness is just as much within reach of you and me today as it was within reach of Stephen. "Jesus Christ is the same yesterday, today and forever" (Hebrews 13:8). What He did, He does. Wherever He has been able to get possession of men as he got possession of Stephen, He begets those same high qualities. Oh, may we not this day, because of the needs of our own lives, because of the needs of our homes, because of the needs of our church, offer ourselves fully to Him. He waits to be gracious. He waits to enter in and possess us. For "we are His witnesses as is also the Holy Ghost, whom God hath given to them that obey Him" (Acts 5:32).

And look a moment at the outcome of this fullness. "Stephen, full of the Holy Spirit, and therefore full of faith and wisdom and power and grace." But what was the end of it all? What did it amount to? The first result of this fullness was not simply that he was a joyous and sunny Christian. He was that. But what we want to notice especially is the effect of his fullness upon the world, upon the people of his own day and the people of all days that have come and are to come after.

Stephen, then, full of the Holy Spirit was full of highest usefulness. He was appointed to a position that looked quiet small. He was to help administer the temporal affairs of a semi-pauper church. But he made these temporal affairs to administer to highest spiritual ends. He gave out bread in such a fashion as to make men hunger for the Bread of Life. And when he passed out a bit of money to the needy, he did not forget to tell them where they could buy wine and milk without money and without price. He worked with his might in his small sphere, and God honored him and made him a mighty preacher.

And how effective he was in his preaching! Jerusalem was a proud and wicked city. It was full of cultured and religious aristocrats. Those aristocrats would have given a world to have been able to ignore Stephen. Nothing would have suited them better than to have been able to treat him with cool and complete contempt. But they could not ignore him. They might as well have tried to ignore a burning building when the wind was high. They might as well have tried to ignore a cyclone. There was hardly a man in Jerusalem stupid enough and sleepy enough not to know that Stephen was in town on a business trip for his King.

Notice, I do not say that everybody welcomed Stephen's message. I do not say that everybody who heard him repented and became a follower of Jesus Christ. Many did. Many even among the priests yielded to his impassioned appeals. Many hearts were softened. But this was not true of all. Some were made only the more bitter. Some had all the serpents within their souls awakened into activity. Some were led to hate him with a hatred that only his life blood could satisfy. But this I say, they could not remain stupidly and stolidly indifferent.

And do I not voice the longing of your heart this morning when I say, Oh, for a church that the world cannot treat with indifference. Oh, for a band of saints that it is absolutely impossible to ignore. Oh, for a ministry that will divide audiences and communities and cities and continents into those who are either out and out for Christ or out and out against Him. Oh, for a Christianity virile enough to compel the active opposition, the open antagonism of the forces of evil that refuse to be won. The church of Jesus Christ can stand any amount of opposition. "The gates of hell shall not prevail against it" (Luke 16:18). But the direst of all dire calamities is for it to become so effete, so powerless, so dead, that it is not worth fighting.

Stephen, full of the Spirit, I repeat, became Stephen, full of highest service. Where he labored, many fell in love with his Lord. Where he labored, opposition grew bitter. His enemies ground their teeth like enraged beasts. But Stephen, with a fine high courage, continued his message. He went on with his sermon, though he knew that every sentence he uttered was becoming a stone in the hands of his enemies. He spoke right on though he knew that he was digging his own grave as he spoke. "Ye stiff-necked and uncircumcised in heart and ears, ye do always resist the Holy Spirit; as your fathers did, so do ye" (Acts 7:51).

The assembly becomes a mob. The young preacher is hurried out of the city. The scene that follows is nothing more than a common lynching. These men have not been able to resist his inspired logic. They have been publicly humiliated. They will have their revenge. And so they pelt him with stones. His angelic face becomes bruised and blood-stained. A few minutes later he lies battered and broken and very still. And the wolves have had their prey.

But they had not been able, with all their stones, to kill his open vision. "I see the heavens open," he cries, "and Jesus standing at the right hand of God" (Acts 7:56). Although they killed his body, they were not able to kill his Christlike spirit of forgiveness. As he falls a victim to their hate, he throws around their cruel shoulders "the sheltering folds of a protecting prayer": "Lord, lay not this sin to their charge" (v. 60). Although they killed his body, they were not able to destroy his peace. "Be quiet," says the mother, as she puts her baby to sleep. But God can put his child to sleep amidst the howl of mobs and the flying of stones. And so Stephen fell asleep.

Stephen, full of the Holy Spirit, was a blessing while he lived. An abiding blessing he has been through all the changing years. One young man stood by that day well pleased with his death. But he was never able to banish the picture of the angelic face of this first Christian martyr from his mind and heart. At last this proud man fell prostrate on the desert sand with this cry upon his lips, "Lord, what wilt thou have me to do?" (Acts 9:6). And I feel confident that the first of the saints Paul greeted when he reached the heavenly country was "Stephen, a man full of the Holy Spirit."

Courage and Enthusiasm

Dwight Lyman Moody (1837-1899) is known around the world as one of America's most effective evangelists. Converted as a teenager through the witness of his Sunday school teacher, Moody became active in YMCA and Sunday school work in Chicago while pursuing a successful business career. He then devoted his life to evangelism and was used mightily of God in campaigns in both the United States and Great Britain. He founded the Northfield School for Girls, the Mount Hermon School for Boys, the Northfield Bible Conference, and the Moody Bible Institute in Chicago. Before the days of planes and radio, Moody traveled more than a million miles and addressed more than 100 million people.

This message is from Dwight L. Moody, in *The Great Pulpit Masters* series, published in 1949 by Fleming H. Revell.

5

COURAGE AND ENTHUSIASM

Be strong and of a good courage (Joshua 1:6, 7, 9, 18).

I SHALL TAKE for my subject tonight only two words, courage and enthusiasm—necessary qualifications for successful work in the Lord's service. In Joshua 1, four different times God tells Joshua to be of good courage; and He says that if he was of good courage no man should be able to stand before him, all the days of his life. Also we read of Joshua that in the evening of his life he was successful, and that no man was able to stand before him all his days. God fulfilled His promise; God kept His word.

But see how careful God is to instruct him on this one point. Four times in one chapter He says to him, "Be of good courage; and then you shall prosper, then you shall have good success." I have yet to find that God ever uses a man that is all the time looking on the dark side, and is all the time talking about the obstacles and looking at them, and is discouraged and cast down. It is not these Christians that go around with their head down like a bulrush, looking at the obstacles and talking about the darkness all the time, that God uses. They kill everything they touch; there is no life in them. Now, if we are going to succeed, we have to be of good courage. The moment we get our eyes on God and remember who He is, that He has all power in heaven and earth, and that it is God who commands us to work in His vineyard, then it is that we will have courage given us.

Two Examples: Moses and Elijah

Now, if you just take your Bibles and look carefully

through them, you will see that men who have left their mark behind them, the men that have been successful in winning souls to Christ, have all been men of that stamp. You will notice that when Moses commenced, after he had been among the Egyptians 40 years, he thought the time had come for him to commence his work of delivering the captives, and he went out. The first thing we hear is that he was looking this way and that way to see is somebody saw him. He was not fit for God's work. God had to take him on the back side of the desert for 40 years. Then God was ready to send him, and Moses then looked but one way. God sent him down into Egypt. Moses had boldness now, and he goes right before the King of Egypt. He had courage, and God could use him. But it took him 40 years to learn this lesson: He must have courage and boldness to be a fit vessel for the Master's use.

Next, we find Elijah on Mount Carmel, full of boldness. How the Lord used him! How the Lord stood by him! How the Lord blessed him! But when he got his eyes off the Lord, and Jezebel sent a message to him that she would have his life, he got afraid. He was not afraid of Ahab and the whole royalty, and he was not afraid of the whole nation. He stood on Mount Carmel alone, and see what courage he had! But what came over him I don't know, unless it was that he got his eyes off the Lord, and when one woman gave him that message he got frightened, and God had to go to him and ask him what he was doing; and he was not fit for God's communion.

Our Trouble

That, I think, is the trouble with a good many of God's people. We get frightened, and we are afraid to speak to men about their souls. We lack moral courage, and if we hear the voice of God speaking to us and saying, "Run and speak to that young man," we will go to him, meaning to do it, yet we will really talk to him about everything else and dare not about his soul. When we begin to invite men to Christ is when the work begins. It won't begin until we have the courage given us and are ready to go and speak with them about their souls. We read that when the apostles were brought before the council, they perceived their boldness; and it made an impression on the council. The Lord could use them then, because they were fearless and bold. Look at Peter on Pentecost, when he charged the murder of the Son of God upon the Jews. A little while before he had got out of communion, and one little maid had scared him nearly out of his life, so that he swore he didn't know Christ. Ah! he had his eyes off the Master, and the moment we get our eyes off Christ we get disheartened; and then God cannot use us.

A Lesson From Noah

I remember a few years ago I got discouraged and could not see much fruit of my work. One morning, as I was in my study, cast down, one of my Sunday school teachers came in and wanted to know what I was discouraged about. I told him it was because I could see no result from my work. Speaking about Noah, he said, "By the way, did you ever study up the chapter of Noah?" I felt that I knew all about that, and I told him that I was familiar with it. He said, "Now, if you never studied that carefully, you ought to do it; for I cannot tell you what a blessing it has been to me."

When he went out, I took down my Bible and commenced to read about Noah; and the thought came stealing over me: "Here is a man that toiled and worked 100 years and didn't get discouraged. If he did, the Holy Spirit didn't put it on record." The clouds lifted; and I got up and said, "If the Lord wants me to work without any fruit I will work on." I went down to the noon prayer meeting; and when I saw the people coming to pray, I said to myself: "Noah worked 100 years, and he never saw a prayer meeting outside of his own family." Pretty soon a man got up right across the aisle where I was sitting and said he had come from a little town where there had been 100 people uniting with the church of God the year before. And I thought to myself: "What if Noah had heard that! He preached so many, many years and didn't get a convert; yet he was not discouraged." Then a man got up right behind me, and he trembled as he said, "I am lost; I want you to pray for my soul." And I said, "What if Noah had heard that! He worked 120 years, and he never had a man come to him and say that; and yet he didn't get discouraged." And I made up my mind then that, God helping me, I would never get discouraged. I would do the best I could and leave the results with God; and it has been a wonderful help to me.

So let me say to the Christians of New York that we must expect good results and never get discouraged; but if we don't get good results, let us not look on the dark side, but keep on praying, and in the fullness of time the blessing of God will come. What we want is to have the Christians come out and take their stand. I find a great many professed Christians for a long time ashamed to acknowledge that they have been quickened. Some have said they did not like the idea of asking Christians to rise, as I did last evening; that it was putting them in a false position. Now, if we are going to be successful, we have got to take our stand for God and let the world and everyone know we are on the Lord's side.

I have great respect for the women that started out during the war with a poker. She heard the enemy were coming and went to resist them. When someone asked her what she could do with a poker, she said she would at least let them know what side she was on. That is what we want, and the time is coming when the line must be drawn in this city, and those on Christ's side must take their stand; and the moment we come out boldly and acknowledge Christ, then it is that men will begin to inquire what they must do to be saved.

A Little Enthusiasm

Then there is a class of people that are not warm

enough. I don't think a little enthusiasm would hurt the church at the present time. I think we need it. I know the world will cry out against it; business men will cry out against religious enthusiasm. But let railroad stocks go up 15 or 20 percent, and see what a revival there would be in business. If there should be a sudden advance in stock, see if there wouldn't be enthusiasm at the Exchange tomorrow. Let there be a sudden change in business, and see if there isn't a good deal of enthusiasm on the street. We can have enthusiasm in business; we can have enthusiasm in politics, and no one complains of that. A man can have enthusiasm in everything else; but the moment that a little fire gets into the church they raise the cry, "Ah, enthusiasm—false excitement—I am afraid of it." I do not want false excitement; but I do think we want a little fire, a little holy enthusiasm. But these men will raise the cry, "Zeal without knowledge." I had a good deal rather have zeal without knowledge than knowledge without zeal; and it won't hurt us to have a little more of this enthusiasm and zeal in the Lord's work.

I saw more zeal when I was in Princeton last Sunday than I have in many a year. I was talking with the students there about their souls, and after I had been talking for some time, quite a group of young men gathered around me; and the moment that one of them made a surrender and said, "Well, I will accept Christ," it seemed as if there were twenty-five hands pressed right down to shake hands with him. That is what we want—men that will rejoice to hear to the conversion of men. Although I don't admire his ideas, I do admire the enthusiasm of that man Garibaldi. It is reported that when he marched toward Rome in 1867, they took him up and threw him into prison, and he sat right down and wrote to his comrades: "If fifty Garibaldis are thrown into prison, let Rome be free!" That is the spirit. Who is Garibaldi? That is nothing. "If fifty Garibaldis are thrown into prison, let Rome be free!" That is what we want in the cause of Christ. We have got to work, and not be loitering at our ease. And then the question of dignity comes up. We have got to lay all that aside, and we have got to be helpers. What difference does it made whether we are hewers of wood or carriers of water, while the temple of God is being erected? Yes, let us have an enthusiasm in the church of God. If we had it in a few of the churches in New York, I believe it would be like a resurrection. The people would say: "What has come over this man? he ain't like the same man he was 2 months ago." We want to have them say: "The Son of God is dearer to us then our money. The Son of God is dearer to us than our families. The Son of God is dearer to us than our position in society."

Let us do anything that the work of God may go on; and when we get there, God will bless us. Why, it says in the Bible, "One shall chase a thousand" (Deuteronomy 32:30). We have not got many of that kind in our churches; I wish we had more of them. It says, "Two shall put ten thousand to flight." Now, if a few should lay hold of God in this way, see what a great army soon will be saved in this city! But, then, we have got to be men after God's own heart. We cannot be lukewarm. We have got to be on fire with the cause of Christ. We have got to have more of this enthusiasm that will carry us into the Lord's work. If there is going to be a great revival in New York, it ain't going to be in this hall. It has got to be done by one and by another going around and talking to their neighbors. There isn't a skeptic, there isn't a drunkard, but what can be reclaimed, if we come with desire in our hearts. We mustn't go around professionally if we want to see any result.

There is a story told in history, in the ninth century, I believe, of a young man that came up with a little handful of men to attack a king who had a great army of 3,000 men. The young man had only 500; and the king sent a messenger to the young man, saying that he need not fear to surrender, for he would treat him mercifully. The young man called up one of his soldiers and said, "Take this dagger and drive it to your heart." The soldier took the dagger and drove it to his heart. Calling up another, he said to him, "Leap into yonder chasm." And the man leaped into the chasm. The young man then said to the messenger:

"Go back and tell your king I have got 500 men like these. We will die, but we will never surrender. And tell your king another thing, that I will have him chained with my dog inside of a few hours." And when the king heard that, he did not dare to meet them, and his army fled before them like chaff before the wind. Within 24 hours he had that king chained with his dog.

That is the kind of zeal we want. "We will die, but we will never surrender." We will work until Jesus comes; and then we will rise with Him. Oh, if men are willing to die for patriotism, why can they not have the same zeal for Christ? All that Abraham Lincoln had to do was to call for men, and how speedily they came. When he called for 600,000 men, how quickly they sprang up all over the nation. Aren't souls worth more than this republic? Aren't souls worth more than this government? Don't we want 600,000 men? If 600 men should come forward, whose hearts were right red-hot for the Son of God, we would be able to see what mighty results would follow. "One man shall chase a thousand, and two shall put ten thousand to flight" (Deuteronomy 32:30).

During our war, the generals that were all the time on the defensive never succeeded. The generals that were successful were the generals that were on the aggressive. Some of our churches think they are doing remarkably well if they hold their membership; and they think, if they have thirty or forty conversions in that church during the year, that that is remarkable work. They think it is enough to supply the places of those who have died, and of those who have wandered away during the past. It seems to me we ought to bring thousands and thousand to Christ. I say the time has come for us to have a war on the side of aggression.

There may be barriers in our path, but God can remove them. There may be a mountain in our way, but God can take us over the mountain. There may be difficulties in the way, but He can overcome them. Our God is above them all; and if the church of God is ready to advance, all obstacles will be removed. No man ever sent by God ever failed, but self must be lost sight of. We must be willing to lay down our lives for the cause of Christ.

When I was going to Europe in 1867, my friend Mr. Stuart, of Philadelphia, said, "Be sure to be at the General Assembly in Edinburgh, in June. I was there last year," said he, "and it did me a world of good." He said that a returned missionary from India was invited to speak to the General Assembly on the needs of India. This old missionary, after a brief address, told the pastors who were present to go home and stir up their churches, and send young men to India to preach the gospel. He spoke with such earnestness that after a while he fainted, and they carried him from the hall. When he recovered, he asked where he was, and they told him the circumstances under which he had been brought there. "Yes," he said, "I was making a plea for India, and I didn't quite finish my speech, did I?" After being told that he did not, he said, "Well, take me back and let me finish it." But they said, "No, you will die in the attempt." "Well," said he, "I will die if I don't." And the old man asked again that they allow him to finish his plea. When he was taken back, the whole congregation stood as one man; and as they brought him on the platform, with a trembling voice, he said, "Fathers and mothers of Scotland is it true that you will not let your sons go to India? I spent 25 years of my life there; I lost my health, and I have come back with sickness and shattered health. If it is true that we have no strong grandsons to go the India, I will pack up what I have and be off tomorrow; and I will let those heathen know that if I cannot live for them, I will die for them."

The world will say that that old man was

enthusiastic. Well, that is just what we want. No doubt
that is what they said of the Son of God, when He was
down here. Oh, that God may baptize us with the spirit
of enthusiasm! That He may anoint us tonight with
the Holy Spirit! Let me say to some of you men—I see
some gray locks here, who, I have no doubt, are saying:
"I wish I was young again; I would like to help in this
work; I would like to work for the Lord." When we
went to London there was an old woman 85 years old
who came to the meetings and said she wanted a hand
in that work. She was appointed to a district, and she
called on all classes of people. She went to places where
we would probably have been put out, and she told the
people of Christ. There were none that could resist
her. When the old woman of 85 years old came to them
and offered to pray for them, they all received her
kindly—Catholics, Jews, Gentiles, all. That is
enthusiasm—that is what we want in New York. If
you cannot give a day to this work, give an hour; or if
not an hour, five minutes. If you have not strength to
do anything personally, you can pray for this work.
Now, it is a good deal better to do that than it is to
stand off criticising. Some will say: "Oh, I heard my
grandfather say how such things should be done. This
is not managed right to be successful." And they stand
off and criticise and find fault; and we will never succeed
as long as they do this. All should work, and ask God's
guidance.

Cheering Others On

Once, when a great fire broke out at midnight, and
people thought that all the inmates had been taken
out, away up there in the fifth story was seen a little
child crying for help. Up went a ladder, and soon a
fireman was seen ascending to the spot. As he neared
the second story, the flames burst in fury from the
windows; and the multitude almost despaired of the
rescue of the child. The brave man faltered, and a
comrade at the bottom cried out, "Cheer!" Cheer upon
cheer arose from the crowd. Up the ladder he went,

and saved the child, because they cheered him. If you cannot go into the heat of the battle yourself, if you cannot go into the harvest field and work day after day, you can cheer those that are working for the Master. I see many old people in their old days get crusty and sour, and they discourage everyone they meet by their fault-finding. That is not what we want. If we made a mistake, come and tell us of it, and we will thank you. You don't know how much you may do by just speaking kindly to those that are willing to work.

I remember when I was a boy, I went several miles from home with an older brother. That seemed to me the longest visit of my life. It seemed that I was then further away from home than I have ever been before, or have ever been since. While we were walking down the street, we saw an old man coming toward us, and my brother said, "There is a man that will give you a cent. He gives every new boy that come into this town a cent." That was my first visit to the town. When the old man got opposite to us, he looked around. My brother, not wishing me to lose the cent, and to remind the old man that I had not received it, told him I was a new boy in the town. The old man, taking off my hat, placed his trembling hand on my head and told me I had a Father in heaven. It was a kind, simple act, but I fell the pressure of the old man's hand upon my head today.

Now, you can all do something in this work of saving souls—that is what we have come to this city for. There is not a mother, father, nor wife, there is not a young man in all the city, but what ought to be in sympathy with this work. We have come here to try to save souls. I never heard of one that was brought to Christ that it injured them. Oh, let us pray for the Spirit of God. Let us pray that this spirit of criticism and fault-finding may be all laid aside, and that we may be of one spirit, as they were on the Day of Pentecost.

NOTES

Ambassadors for Christ

William E. Sangster (1900-1960) was the "John Wesley" of his generation as he devoted his life to evangelism and the promotion of practical sanctification. He pastored in England and Wales, and his preaching ability attracted the attention of the Methodist leaders. He ministered during World War II at Westminister Central Hall, London, where he pastored the church, managed an air-raid shelter in the basement, and studied for his Ph.D. at the London University. He served as president of the Methodist Conference (1950) and director of the denomination's home missions and evangelism ministry. He published several books on preaching, sanctification, and evangelism, as well as volumes of sermons.

This message comes from *Westminster Sermons,* Volume 1, published in 1960 by The Epworth Press, London.

William E. Sangster

6

AMBASSADORS FOR CHRIST

We are ambassadors for Christ, as though God did beseech
you by us: we pray you in Christ's stead, be ye reconciled
to God (2 Corinthians 5:20).

DID YOU EVER read that remarkable book called
Ambassador on Special Mission? It was written by Lord
Templewood, still best known to most people as Sir
Samuel Hoare. It tells the story of his dispatch to Spain
at a most critical period of World War II with
instructions to keep Franco out of the struggle, and it
tells something also of the adventures which befell him
in that difficult task.

As I followed the twists and turns of fortune and of
policy, and sensed again the privileges and
responsibilities of the ambassador's life, I remembered
once more this striking word of Paul's, "We are
ambassadors for Christ" and I would like to examine
that word with you this morning.

Ambassador Defined

Everybody knows—even the least informed—that an
ambassador is one who *represents his own country in
an alien land.* If his country is a monarchy, the
ambassador is regarded as the personal representative
of the king (or queen), and it is expected that he will
be accredited the honors and distinctions which
belong—not to him as a person—but to the one in whose
place he stand.

Not only is the ambassador regarded as the personal
representative of his king, but his official residency—
the embassy—is always accounted as belonging, not to
the country in which it is built, but to the country to
which the ambassador himself belongs. The British

Embassy in Washington is a little bit of Britain. The American Embassy in London is a precious scrap of the United States.

Within the walls of an embassy only those rules and customs and laws are observed which belong to the land of the ambassador; the laws and the customs of the alien land in which he lives pass unheeded by. When America went "dry", there was still wine on the table of the British ambassador in Washington—and the Ambassador was not breaking the law. Britain had not gone dry! On the fourth Thursday of every November, there is a wonderful party at the American Embassy in Grosvenor Square in London because it is Thanksgiving Day. But Thanksgiving Day has no place in the British calendar, and all round the rest of the Mayfair it is just—November!

An ambassador's allegiance is to his own land and his own king. He dwells as a Britisher (or American) *in* Spain, or Portugal, or in the Argentine, but he is not *of* it. His citizenship, and his loyalty, and his love are all elsewhere.

"Now," says Paul *"we* are ambassadors for Christ."

Ambassadors! Personal representatives of our heavenly King.

> Chosen to be soldiers
> In an alien land.

And more than soldiers—ambassadors!

> Chosen, called, and faithful,
> For our Captain's band.

Is that true? Are you living up to your ambassadorial status?

No one sensitive to the importance of rank can ever speak lightly of the ambassadorial status. It is, in all conscience, a tremendous thing to be the personal representative of a great Ruler and to speak for your whole land.

Would you like to have been the Ambassador of Britain to Turkey when the poor Samaritans were being exterminated, and to have told the Sultan to his face,

"My Queen won't stand aside and see this little people wiped out"? There are Samaritans in the world today because our ambassador said that!

Would you like to have been the ambassador of Britain to Portugal after the dreadful disaster at Lisbon in 1755, and to have said to the King of Portugal, "My King commands me to convey his deep compassion to you and to your people, and to give you £40,000 to alleviate the distress?"

It is high office, the office of an ambassador. Are you living up to your status? *Are you really an ambassador of Jesus Christ?*

And tell me this.

Is your home an ambassy of heaven?

That is what Paul asked his loved Philippians when he wrote to them. Philippi had the distinction of being a Roman colony with all the privileges which that status carried in the ancient world, but Paul wanted the church at Philippi to be a colony of heaven.

Is this church, so far as you can make it, a colony of heaven? Is your home, so far as you can make it, an embassy of Jesus Christ? Do *His* rules and customs and laws alone prevail within its walls? Is service the motive, and peace the atmosphere, and joy the sunshine, and love the whole reward? If some discerning soul called on you at home, would he say within himself, "This is an embassy of Jesus Christ?"

The Ambassador's Access

Now an ambassador always has, as one of his jealously guarded privileges, *direct access to the king (or President) he represents.* How could he possibly represent his king unless he knew his monarch's mind?

Consequently, it is the established practice among all civilized communities that maintain ambassadors in the capital cities of other powers, to guarantee to every ambassador uninterrupted communication with those he represents.

Our post office carries the diplomatic mailbag of every

ambassador accredited to the Court of St. James, but never, on the solemn word of Britain, is that mail-bag ever opened and explored. It cannot be tampered with by the Civil Service, nor by Scotland Yard, nor by the customs and excise authorities, nor by any others.

The same respect is paid to the mailbags of our own ambassadors abroad. They are sealed at the foreign office and, with the seal unbroken, they are delivered in Paris, Brussels, Rome, Madrid, and wheresoever else our ambassadors reside.

No man would accept his high office if he were not guaranteed uninterrupted communication with his king.

The Christian ambassador is guaranteed no less. When Jesus Christ makes us ambassadors, He promises us that indispensable privilege. He says, "You are going to represent Me in an alien world. You may always know My mind. Nothing need ever interrupt our intercourse, *but your neglect or indifference.* When you pray I will hear; when you listen I will speak. Nothing external to yourself can ever cut our communications. You may always know the mind of your King."

So the Christian ambassadors have proved all through the ages. They flung John Bunyan into prison— but they couldn't cut his communications. In prison he prayed and God heard him. In prison God spoke and Bunyan knew his King's mind.

George Fox and John Nelson and Samuel Rutherford and a thousand others have been incarcerated in jail for Christ's sake, but they all testify that the mail arrived from heaven; they had sweet communion with their King.

I was speaking once to one of our boys recently home from the war. He was telling me—what I knew by experience already—of the problems of living the Christian life in the services.

"The secret of success," he said, "is in prayer. If I could get away for a quiet time; if I could speak to God and listen to God . . . all was well."

That is the secret of success in the ambassadorial service anywhere and at any time.

Do you know why so many people fail as Christian ambassadors? They don't maintain communication with their King.

The Danger of Being an Ambassador

But Lord Templewood, in his recent book, stressed something else beside that. He said that if an ambassador stays too long in the country to which he is accredited—that is to say, if he does not make fairly frequent visits to his own land and breathe his own native air—he gets "denationalized."

The process can go on, it seems, without the ambassador being fully aware of it. When he first arrives on his mission, he is British or American through and through. To the discerning eye, "made in England" or "made in America" is written all over his face. He sees things his own way, assesses them from his own standpoint, is able—even in a land of dictators—to see things always from the democratic angle.

But, half-unconsciously, there supervenes a cosmopolitan way of looking at things. The atmosphere of the alien land gets into his lungs. Whenever he goes out, he meets people of *that* land. Whenever he talks, he hears the viewpoint of *those* people expressed. Bit by bit—and almost imperceptibly at first—his attitude is affected; it begins to change. From British or American it becomes cosmopolitan, pro-Spanish or Italian or Brazilian—whatever the country may be.

The problem of every ambassador, if he is to remain loyal to his commission, is to be true all the time to his prime allegiance.

And Lord Templewood says that if he is to do that, he must "renew his strength by contact with his native soil," breathe his own atmosphere, talk with his own kind, and get truly orientated again from the center.

And how true that is of the Christian.

No man or woman can hope to be a dependable ambassador of Jesus Christ unless he or she maintains his prime allegiance. The alien world in which we live affects us all. We are in it nearly all the time. Its judgments affect us; its atmosphere penetrates us; its pressures bear on us in ten thousand ways.

How easily, without realizing it, do we become what the apostle calls "conformed to this world" (Romans 12:2). How easily we accept a lower standard; take to saying: "Well, I see no harm in it"; lose the sharp distinction between right and wrong; have all our blacks and whites dissolve into one indeterminate grey; keep up the pretence of being ambassadors by preserving one or two Christians customs, but—for the rest—we are unworthy; quite definitely not true to our ambassadorial status; something of a failure; a casualty of the diplomatic service.

Is that true of you? Dare you say with Paul, "I am an ambassador for Christ"?

How can one save oneself from being what Sir Samuel Hoare calls "denationalized" and what, in this connection, I may call "despiritualized"? By what means can a man be on his guard against that possibility?

You must do what Hoare did. You must get back whenever you can to your own atmosphere. You must mingle, at *every* opportunity, with your own kind. You must guard not only your own mailbag—by which I mean those secret communications you may have in private prayer and in listening to God—but you must also keep in the Christian fellowship. Be found *often* in the sanctuary. Count Sunday to Sunday too long in the atmosphere of the world and seek a meeting of fellowship or prayer in the mid-week.

I believe that ambassadors *can* retain their true citizenship in this alien world without those meetings of mid-week fellowship if they are always jealously guarding their periods of daily prayer, and if it is quite impossible for them to get to those mid-week meetings at all.

But if you are serious to maintain your ambassadorial status, and if it *is* possible for you to get to a weekday class or Christian fellowship meetings or prayer group . . . Oh, I beg of you, be there. Be there!

Ambassador on a Special Mission

You will remember that I remarked, as I began, that Lord Templewood described himself as "*an ambassador on special mission.*" He was not an *ordinary* ambassador. His King set him a specific task.

We were at a grim phase of the war. Britain was hard-pressed. She was, indeed, alone in the fight against tyranny. The Nazis were supreme from the Pyrénées to Russia, and some, even of our staunch American friends, doubted if we could possibly hold out.

Franco was known to be pro-Nazi and pro-Fascist. He made no secret of it himself. He identified himself with those evil régimes and openly announced himself as simply "non-belligerent."

Sir Samuel Hoare, in that hour of need, was sent to keep him out of the war; to prevent him coming in militantly on the side of the Axis, for if the Germans had swept down the Iberian Peninsula, how would it have gone with the handful of men on the Rock of Gibraltar, who would have had but little choice except to sell their lives dearly, and see the Mediterranean sealed at its western end?

Those of us who followed events closely in those days felt almost sure, during some months, that Franco would come in against us.

He never came in against us! Let Sir Samuel Hoare have his credit for that. He set himself the task of understanding the Spanish mind, of thinking their thoughts before them, of putting our case and keeping them out.

He was, indeed, an ambassador on special mission. It would have gone ill with Britain if Spain had come in against us then.

We, as Christian ambassadors, have a special mission too. Indeed, none so special as we are!

Remember the whole text. This is how Paul put it: "Now then we are ambassadors for Christ, as though God did beseech you by us; we pray you in Christ's stead, be ye reconciled to God."

"Be ye reconciled to God"! What a task! Have you felt the critical character and all the responsibility and importance of your mission as ambassadors of reconciliation?

I said just now that Sir Samuel Hoare studied the Spanish mind—and Franco's in particular. He was very lonely, the embassy was sometimes mobbed and he had no firm friend but the American ambassador—so he concentrated the more on the Spanish mind.

Do you study the minds of people outside the Church—and in particular, the people you know?

Hoare had to ask himself, "What do they want? What do they fear? How can I put my point of view in such a way that they will follow my counsel?"

Do you ask those things about the worldling? "What does want? What does he fear? How can I put my plea in such a way that he himself will want to be reconciled to God?"

When he says to you, "I want to get a kick out of life; I want to be happy", do you know how to tell him about a joy that never fades away; happiness that has no hangover? Can you tell him about that?

When he says that he wants satisfaction, and he thinks that the way to satisfaction is to give his animal desires whatever they want whenever they want it, do you know how to convince him that that is the way to a troubled conscience, and that only in God can he find a peace that endures?

I am asking you *this,* in short; do you know the craft of this ambassadorial skill in personal evangelism? Can you clear misunderstandings from the unbeliever's mind and tell him convincingly and without embarrassment: "I am from God. Oh yes! I hold that status. I am an ambassador of the King of kings. I have been commissioned from above. I am accredited to this alien world. I have letters to prove my ambassadorial status. The King I represent wants a reconciliation with you. Though He is the offended One, He takes the initiative, and He wants me to tell you that there are no barriers in Him to that reconciliation. Whatever barriers there

are, are all in *you.* If you want to be right with Him,
you can. He has provided the way Himself. Accept the
atonement of His only begotten Son. Put yourself within
the newly covenanted mercies. Regularize your position
in relation to heaven. He has pardon for you. Take the
pardon. Be reconciled to God"?

You wouldn't use that *language.* You would adapt it
to the person you were addressing, but there would be
no blurring of the sense. Your "special mission" is to
get them reconciled to God and you would have to take
as direct a line to the end as you could.

What a mission! Oh, the privilege and wonder of
being able to say it; of being able to say it to *anybody;*
to know that it is for all—the foulest; the most inferior;
the man who has murdered his mother even....

Tell it out! You are an ambassador. Tell it out! Live
up to your ambassadorial status. Spend your days that
way.

'Tis worth living for this,
To administer bliss
And salvation in Jesus's name.

Calling the Ambassador Home

*Sooner or later every ambassador is relieved of his
post.* He is called home. Sir Samuel Hoare was called
home. His task had been well done. The King told him
so, Sir Winston Churchill said so, and the discerning
public said so too.

But doubtless it was the King's word that meant the
most to him. And it was not a word of thanks only. He
was rewarded. He was given a peerage and a place by
the throne. The King said, in effect: "When the court is
in session, stand here; stand by the throne. The work
was well done and I am well pleased."

Some day the Christian ambassador will be called
Home. God doesn't intend that he dwell forever in an
alien land. Some day that call will come to you and to
me. Suddenly perhaps . . . or with warning. It is as the
Monarch wills. When it comes, may it only find us

fulfilling our ambassadorial duties; busy in the tasks He has given; filling the moments with glad service to Him.

Last Thursday, in the town of Stockton-on-Tees, I went into a house to see an old ambassador of Jesus Christ waiting for his call home. He had been warned. I have known him for years. What an ambassador he has been! They know my friend along Tees-side. Eighty-eighty last week, but he has not been out of his room for a year, and, as I leaned over his bed, I said to him (remembering a favorite hymn) with a twinkle in my eye: "Is it well with thy soul?"

And he replied firmly and smilingly, "It is *well*; it is WELL with my soul."

He is waiting to be called home, that ambassador. He feels an unprofitable servant, but he sees also the smile of his King. He is not afraid. He is just waiting for the call.

Will it be like that with you some day? You hope to die in your bed, and have time enough to recollect yourself before the journey is begun.

That is how I hope it will be with me. I hope, when He comes for me, that in some way or other I may be discharging my ambassadorial duties, and for myself and for you I would say:

> O that each in the day
> Of His coming may say:
> I have fought my way through,
> I have finished the work Thou didst give me to do!

> O that each from his Lord
> May receive the glad word:
> Well and faithfully done;
> *Enter into My joy, and sit down by My throne!*

NOTES

Some Features of Christ's Working

George H. Morrison (1866-1928) assisted the great
Alexander Whyte in Edinburgh, pastored two churches,
and then became pastor in 1902 of the distinguished
Wellington Church on University Avenue in Glasgow,
Scotland. His preaching drew great crowds; in fact,
people had to line up an hour before the services to be
sure to get seats in the large auditorium. Morrison is a
master of imagination in preaching; yet his messages
are solidly biblical.

From his many volumes of sermons, I have chosen
this message, found in *Flood-Tide,* published 1904 by
Hodder and Stoughton, London.

George H. Morrison

7

SOME FEATURES OF CHRIST'S WORKING

My Father worketh hitherto, and I work (John 5:17).

IT IS CHARACTERISTIC of the Christian gospel that its Savior should be a worker. In the old world, it was hardly an honorable thing to work. It was a thing for slaves, and serfs, and strangers, not for freeborn men. Hence work and greatness rarely went together, and nothing could be more alien to the genius of paganism than a toiling God. Jesus has changed all that. He has made it impossible for us to think of God as indolent. It was a revolution when Jesus taught "God loves." But it was hardly less revolutionary when He taught "God works."

And He not only taught it, He lived it too. Men saw in Christ a life of endless toil, and "he that hath seen Me hath seen the Father" (John 14:9). Had Jesus lived and taught in the quiet groves of some academy, it would have made all the difference in the Christian view of work, and all the difference in the Christian view of God. But Jesus was a carpenter. And Jesus stooped to the very humblest tasks till He became the pattern and prince of workers. I want to look, then, at some features of His work tonight. For He has left us an example that we should follow in His steps.

His Purpose; His Methods

Looking back, then, upon the work of Jesus, what strikes me first is the magnitude of His aim compared with the meanness of His methods.

It is a great thing to command an army. It is a great thing to be the master of a fleet. It is a great thing to be a minister of state, and help to guide a people toward their national destiny. But the aims of general, and of admiral, and of statesman, great in themselves, seem almost insignificant when we compare them with the purposes of Jesus. He claims a universal sovereignty. He runs that sovereignty out into every sphere. His is to be the test in moral questions. He is to shape our law and mold our literature. He is the Lord of life. He is the king and conqueror of death. These are the purposes of Jesus, far more stupendous than man had ever dreamed of in his wildest moments. Will He not need stupendous methods if He is ever to achieve an aim like that?

And it is then the apparent meanness—the ordinariness—of His methods strikes us. Had He a pen of fire? He never wrote a line, save in the sand. Had He a voice of overmastering eloquence? He would not strive, nor cry, nor lift up His voice in the streets. Was there unlimited wealth at His command?—"The foxes have holes, and the birds of the air have nests, but the Son of Man hath not where to lay His head" (Matthew 8:20). Were His first followers men of influence?—"Simon and Andrew were casting a net into the sea, for they were fishers" (Matthew 4:18). Or would He use the sword like Mohammed?—"Put up thy sword into its place. He that taketh the sword shall perish by the sword" (Matthew 25:52). It seems impossible that in such ways Christ should achieve His purpose. It is the magnitude of His aim compared with the meanness of His methods that arrests me first.

It should be so with every Christian toiler. It is a simple lesson for every man and woman who seeks to serve in the true Christian spirit. Surrounded by the ordinary, he should be facing heavenwards. Poorly equipped in all things else, he should be mightily equipped in noble hope. If I am Christ's, I cannot measure possibilities by methods. My heaven is always greater than my grasp. If I am Christ's, I cherish the loftiest hope, and I am content to work for it in lowliest ways.

And it is there the difference comes in between a visionary and a Christian. A visionary dreams his dreams and builds his castles in the air. They are radiant and wonderful and golden and the light of heaven glitters on every minaret. And then, because he cannot realize them *now,* and cannot draw them in all their beauty down to earth, the visionary folds his hands, does nothing, and the vision goes. But the true Christian, with hopes as glorious as any visionary's, because they are the hopes of Jesus Christ, carries the glory of them into his common duty and into the cross-bearing of the dreary day. And though the generations die, and the purposes of God take a thousand years to ripen, he serves and is content—

> Jesus *shall* reign where'er the sun
> Doth his successive journeys run.

Untiring Labor; Unruffled Calm

Once more, as I look back upon the work of Jesus, I find there untiring labor joined with unruffled calm.

There never was a ministry, whether of man or angel, so varied, so intense, or so sustained as was the public ministry of Jesus. He preaches in the synagogue at Nazareth. He preaches on the hill and on the sea. With infinite patience and unexhausted tenderness he trains the Twelve. And all that we know of Him is not a thousandth part of what He said and did. Charged with that mighty task, and with only three short years to work it out, shall we not find Christ anxious? And will we not light on hours of feverish unrest? There is no trace of that. With all its stir, no life is so restful as the life of Jesus. With all its incident and crowding of event, we are amazed at the supreme tranquillity of Christ. There is time for teaching and there is time for healing. There is time for answering and time for prayer. Each hour is full of work and full of peace. No day hands on its debts to tomorrow. Jesus can cry, "It is finished" (John 19:30), at the close. Here for each worker is the supreme example of untiring labor and unruffled calm.

Let us remember that. It is the very lesson that we need today. There are two dangers that, in these bustling times, beset the busy man. One is that he be so immersed in multifarious business that all the lights of heaven are blotted out. The calm and quietness that are our heritage as Christians are put to flight in the unceasing round. Life lacks its unity, loses its central plan, becomes a race and not a stately progress, and slackens its grasp upon eternal things till we grow fretful in the constant pressure. Then men who looked to us, as followers of Jesus, for a lesson, find us as worried and anxious as themselves. That is the one extreme: it is the danger of the practical mind. But then there is the other: it is the mystic's danger. It is that, realizing the utter need of fellowship with God, a man should neglect the tasks that his time brings him, and should do nothing because there is so much to do. All mysticism tends to that. It is a recoil from an exaggerated service. It is the shutting of the ear to the more clamorous calls, so that we may hear more certainly the still small voice.

But all that is noblest in the mystic's temper, and all that is worthiest in the man of deeds, mingled and met in the service of our Lord. Here is the multitude of tasks. Here is the perfect calm. That is the very spirit we need to rebaptize our service of today. God in the life means an eternal purpose and work achieved on the line of an eternal purpose is work without friction and duty without fret. God in the life means everlasting love and to realize an everlasting love is to experience unutterable peace.

Mission for All; Message for Each

As I look back upon Christ's work, there is yet another feature of it that strikes me. I find in it a mission for all joined with a message for each.

Times without number we find Jesus surrounded by a multitude. Christ is the center of many crowds. Wherever He is, the crowd is sure to gather. And how

He was stirred, and moved, and filled with compassion for the multitude, all readers of the gospel story know. Every chord of His human heart was set a-vibrating by a vast assembly. The common life of congregated thousands touched Him, true man, to all his heights and depths. He fed them, taught them. This was His parting charge, "Go ye into all the world and preach!" (Mark 16:18). Yet for all this—the wide sweep of His mission—no teacher ever worked on so minute a scale as Jesus Christ. Did any crowd ever get deeper teaching than Nicodemus when he came alone? And was the woman of Samaria despised because companionless? How many sheep did the shepherd go to seek when the ninety and nine were in the fold? How many pieces of silver had gone lost? How many sons came home from the far country before the father brought out his robes and killed the calf? Christ did not work on the scale of a thousand, or on the scale of ten, but on the scale of one. Companionless men were born, and companionless they must be born again.

Brethren, we must remember that. We cannot afford, in these days, when all the tendency is toward the statistics of the crowd—we cannot afford to despise that great example. It is true, there is a stimulus in numbers. There is an indescribable sympathy that runs like an electric thrill through a great gathering; and heights of eloquence and song and prayer are sometimes reached where the crowd is, that never could have been reached in solitude. But for all that, all Christlike work is on the scale of one. Jesus insists on quality, not quantity. And when the books are opened and the strange story of the past is read, some voices that the world never heard, as of a mother or a friend, shall be found more like Christ's than others that have thrilled thousands by their eloquence.

Pray over that sweet prayer of the Moravian liturgy: "From the desire of being great, good Lord, deliver us." A word may change a life. It did it for the Philippian jailer. A look may soften a hard heart. It did for Peter. To sanctify life's trifles, to redeem the opportunities for good the dullest day affords, never to go to rest without some secret effort to bring but a little happiness to some single heart—men who do this, unnoticed through the unnoticed years, grow Christlike; men who do this shall be amazed to waken *yonder,* and find that they are standing nearer God than preacher or than martyr, if preaching and if martyrdom were all.

Seeming Failure; Signal Triumph

Lastly, as I look back upon that life of Christ, I see another feature. I see in it seeming failure joined with signal triumph. If ever there was a life that seemed to have failed, it was the life of Jesus. For a time it had looked as if triumph had been coming. The people had been awakened. The national hope had begun to center round Him. A little encouragement, and they would have risen in enthusiasm for Messiah. But when Jesus went to His death, all that was changed. The people had deserted Him. His very disciples had forsaken Him and fled. His hopes were shattered, and His cause was lost. His kingdom had been a splendid dream, and Jesus had been the king of visionaries. Now it was over. The cross and the grave were the last act in the great tragedy. Jesus had bravely tried, and He had failed. Yes! so it seemed. Perhaps even to the nearest and the dearest so it seemed. God's hand had written failure over the work of Jesus.

When lo! on the third day, the gates of the grave are burst, and Jesus rises. And the Holy Spirit descends on the apostles, and they begin to preach. And the tidings are carried to the isles, and pierce the continents. And a dying world begins to breathe again: and hope comes back, and purity and honor, and pardon and a new power to live, and a new sense of God, and it all sprang from the very moment when they wagged their heads and said, "He save others, Himself He cannot save" (Matthew 27:42). Failure? not failure— triumph! It was a seeming failure in the eyes of man, it was a signal triumph in the plans of God.

O heart so haunted by the sense of failure, remember that. O worker on whose best efforts, both to do and be, failure seems stamped tonight, remember that. If I have learned anything from the sacred story, it is this, that seeming failure is often true success. When John the Baptist lay in his gloomy prison, it must have seemed to him that he had failed. Yet even then, a voice that never erred was calling him the greatest born of women. When Paul lay bound in Rome, did no sense of failure visit him? Yet there, chained to the soldier, he penned these letters that run like the chariots of Christ. God is the judge of failure, and not you. Leave it to Him, and forward. Successes here are often failures yonder, and failures here are sometimes triumphs there.

One of our Scottish ministers and poets has a short piece he names "A Call to Failure"—

> Have I no calls to failure,
> Have I no blessings for loss,
> Must not the way to the mission
> Lie through the path to the Cross?

But one of our English ministers and poets has a short piece that is a call to triumph—

> He always wins who sides with God,
> No chance to him is lost.

And is the one false, and the other true?
Nay, both and true.

Individuality

John Daniel Jones (1865-1942) served for 40 years at the Richmond Hill Congregational Church in Bournemouth, England, where he ministered the Word with a remarkable consistency of quality and effectiveness, as his many volumes of published sermons attest. A leader in his denomination, he gave himself to church extension (he helped to start 30 new churches), assistance to needier congregations, and increased salaries for the clergy. He spoke at D.L. Moody's Northfield Conference in 1919.

This sermon is from his book, *The Hope of the Gospel,* published in 1911 by Hodder and Stoughton.

J. D. Jones

8

INDIVIDUALITY

And Saul clad David with his apparel, and he put an helmet of brass upon his head, and he clad him with a coat of mail. And David girded his sword upon his apparel, and he assayed to go; for he had not proved it. And David said unto Saul, I cannot go with these, for I have not proved them. And David put them off him (1 Samuel 17:38, 39).

YOU REMEMBER ALL about this old Scripture story. It was only after much persuasion that Saul consented to let David go and fight against Goliath at all. But when once he had given consent, his next care was that David should be properly equipped for the encounter. Now, Saul had only one notion of a soldier's equipment. So he produced for David the coat of mail and the helmet of brass which, apparently, he himself was accustomed to wear, and the heavy sword which he himself was accustomed to wield. But when David put them on, he found Saul's armor an encumbrance, and not a help. It did not fit him. It impeded and hampered his movements. He could not fight in it. So he had the courage to lay aside the helmet and the coat of mail and the heavy sword and to say frankly to the king, "I cannot go with these; for I have not proved them;" and he issued forth to his encounter with Goliath in his simple shepherd's dress, and with only one weapon in his hand—that sling which he so well knew how to use.

Now, it is not about Saul and David and this historic combat that I wish to speak in this sermon. Saul and David are types. Saul stands, shall I say, for the *desire for uniformity*. David stands for the *assertion of individuality*. I want to speak for a few minutes about the necessity of resisting the tendency to uniformity and insisting upon our own individuality if we are to be successful workers and fighters.

The Passion for Uniformity

Look first at Saul's action in the story. Saul had the notion that there was only one method of fighting, and that was the one to which he himself was accustomed. He thought there was only one equipment for war, and that was the regulation equipment of helmet and coat of mail and heavy sword. He thought that Goliath could be fought only by the use of one set of weapons, and those were the weapons he himself employed. And so he sought to dress up David in his own armor. No doubt he did it all in good faith, but it was a foolish thing nevertheless. For what he was really trying to do was this—he was trying to repress David's individuality, and convert him into a second Saul.

In this respect Saul stands for the prevailing tendency and temper of human society. "The virtue in most request in society," says Emerson, "is conformity. Self-reliance is its aversion. It loves not realities and creators, but names and customs." And Emerson has not stated the case a whit too strongly. All the facts of life and experience confirm what he says. The whole tendency of society is to destroy individuality and to produce a level and monotonous uniformity. Every child who comes into this world from the hand of God is unique, an original. But from the moment of his birth all the forces of social life set to work upon that little child to destroy his individuality and turn him out a copy of the approved and recognized type. Society has its forms and conventions and standards, and these it seeks to impose upon every living person. In dress, in speech, in thought, it seeks to reduce men to a common level. Everyone knows how society dislikes the man with new ideas, new methods, new phrases. It distrusts the innovator. It fears the man who dares to be original and individual. The man it loves is the correct, respectable, orthodox person who respects traditions, worships convention, and falls in with established customs and ways.

Now, up to a certain point, respect for the usages and customs and traditions and beliefs of society is right and admirable. For these customs and usages and beliefs are the results of the accumulated experience and knowledge of the centuries. But a blind acceptance of them is fatal to all individuality and to all progress. Illustrations occur to me of attempts which are made even to this day to secure certain kinds of uniformity, with quite disastrous results.

There is often an attempt made to secure a certain uniformity of religious experience. We expect all people to pass through the same processes of religious development, and if they do not pass through what we consider to be the normal and recognized experience, we are more than half inclined to think they are not Christians at all. For instance, a great many think the one and only method of becoming a Christian is by means of the "penitent form," and through that tremendous and radical change which we speak of as *conversion.* So the attempt is often made to force people through this process. They are swept into the inquirer rooms at special missions, and they are often made to confess to experiences that they do not really feel. It is only by passing through these various experiences that we think they can be soundly saved.

But surely there is more than one way of "coming to Christ" and winning the kingdom, and it is foolish and absurd of us to try and insist upon one stereotyped method. Here are two hyacinths in full and perfect bloom. But they came by their perfection and beauty in different ways. One grew in earth, the other in water. Here are two Christian men, both obviously living consecrated lives; one came to Christ, like Paul, through a startling and overwhelming experience; the other came, like Timothy, through the gracious ministries of the home. One son wanders far before he really settles down in the Father's house, another never leaves home at all. In face of the facts of life it is absurd to try to limit the methods of God's working. The Spirit bloweth where it listeth. Our way into the kingdom is not the only way. There are on the north three gates, and on the south three gates, and on the east three gates, and on the west three gates, and by any one of these the redeemed may enter. We sin against the plain teaching of Scripture, and we may do grave and irreparable wrong to souls by insisting upon a uniformity of religious experience.

Just as there are different methods of entering the kingdom, so there are *different types of religious life,* and we make a fatal blunder when we expect the spiritual life in everyone to express itself in the same way. What Saul tried to do in this story was to put a giant's armor upon a boy. We made the same mistake in another sphere when we expect the man's religious experience from the youth. Youth has its own type of religion; manhood has another; old age has yet another; and they are each beautiful in their place. But it is foolish and wicked to expect the grown-up person's religion in the child. Buoyancy and strenuousness are, or ought to be, the marks of a young man's religion; a certain wistful waiting for the beyond is often a touching characteristic of the religion of the old. I can understand the old saint saying—

> I'm kneeling at the threshold,
> A-weary, faint and sore.

But I do not want to hear a young man talk like that. When the young man adopts the phraseology of the old Christian, that is cant. "Rejoice, O young men, in thy youth." There can be no uniformity of religious life, and we simply destroy its naturalness and beauty when we try to run the experience of young and old into the same mold.

It is equally foolish to try to impose the forms of truth accepted in one age upon another. We should never dream of doing this in the realm of secular knowledge. You could not, for instance, make this early part of the twentieth century talk in the scientific language current in the beginning of the nineteenth. We have outgrown the nineteenth. New tracts and continents of knowledge have been discovered as the result of the unremitting researchers of scientists, and multitudes of the ideas and beliefs of a hundred years ago have been cast into the lumber-room of exploded superstitions. So rapidly, indeed, does scientific knowledge advance, that even in a score of years a book becomes out of date. But if we refuse to attempt to make the twentieth century speak the scientific language of the nineteenth century, why should we try to compel it to speak the theological language of centuries long gone by? Religious knowledge enlarges and grows just as certainly as scientific knowledge does. Our Lord Himself said that the Spirit would take of His things and would reveal them unto His people. "The Lord," said our own John Robinson in a golden sentence, "hath still more light and truth to break forth from His Word." And the new light and larger knowledge will inevitably express themselves in new speech. It is nothing less than absurd and foolish to expect the twentieth century to speak the religious language and think the religious thought of the fourth century or the seventeenth. Has the Spirit of Christ not been with us through the centuries that have since elapsed? And has He not been leading us into fuller and larger truth?

Calvin was a great and subtle theologian, but it is foolish, and worse than foolish, to try to make men speak today in the language of Calvin's *Institutes.* The Westminster Confession is a great and notable document; valuable as an expression of the Puritan faith, and useful even now for spiritual purposes, but it is futile to try to make men speak the language and propound the belief of the Westminster Confession. John Wesley was one of God's greatest gifts to England, but it always seems to me, as an outsider, foolish and absurd to try to make modern Methodists speak the eighteenth-century language of Wesley. We should have been spared many a weary controversy and humiliating heresy-hunt if we only realized that knowledge constantly grows from more to more. Creeds are invaluable as marking the successive stages of theological development, but to try to make English religious thought of today speak the language and propound the beliefs of the Westminster Confession is as foolish as Saul's attempt to dress up David and send him forth to fight in an armor that did not fit him.

There is also the attempt which is often made to insist upon uniformity of method. Saul thought there really was only one way of fighting. The bare idea of fighting with a sling and a few smooth stones scandalized him. There was one orthodox method of fighting, and Saul wished to compel David to adopt it. Now, a great many cherish a similar passion for uniformity in Christian work. They feel there can be only one right way of working, and that is the way of which they have been accustomed, and that particular method they would like to constrain every man to follow. History abounds with illustrations of this attempt to enforce uniformity and destroy individuality. In Elizabeth's reign, and again in the reign of Charles II, Acts of Uniformity were passed, the whole object of which was to try to constrain the people of this land all to worship and work in the same way.

Wesley and his first helpers were all of them members of the established church and had no wish to leave it. But when they started their great Revival and took to open-air preaching and society meetings, the members of the established church did all they could to thwart and strangle the movement and drive Wesley and his friends back into the old grooves, the respectable, recognized methods of religious work.

And we need not even go back to the beginning of the Methodist movement, for in General Booth's experience we have an illustration of very much the same kind of thing. William Booth was a New Connexion minister. He did not wish to leave the Connexion. But the Connexion had no room for him. With its veneration for rules and traditions it wished to make this man, whose soul was all aflame with a great passion for evangelistic work, tread the humdrum path of the circuit ministry. It wanted no individuality, and so William Booth came out and founded that marvelous Army, which has won such triumphs in every quarter of the world.

And may I not add that this is the tragic mistake that the churches are making in their several attitudes towards each other? There is an astonishing veneration for uniformity—uniformity of method and organization. "Master," said one of His disciples to Jesus one day, "we saw one casting out devils in Thy name, and we forbade him because he followeth not with us" (Luke 9:49). The man was doing good work, holy work, saving work, but that disciple wanted to stop him simply and solely on a point of method—"because he followeth not with us." And is not that typical of what the churches are doing to one another?

I do not desire to speak bitterly—it is not matter for bitterness, but rather for sorrow and regret—but is not that exactly what the Romanist does to the Anglican? He pronounces his orders invalid; he says he has no right to teach and preach—and all because "he followeth not with us." And, in turn, is that not exactly what the Anglican does to the Free Churchman? It is all very pitiable and very deplorable, and utterly mistaken and false. Jesus refused to forbid that irregular and unorthodox worker. Uniformity was no idol of our Lord's. He knew there were diversities of operations, but the same spirit. And it is foolish, and worse than foolish, to try and insist upon uniformity of method and organization today. Men have their individual temperaments and tastes. One man finds himself happier with the more elaborate organization of the Episcopal Church; another finds himself more at home in the freer life of these churches of ours: one man worships best by the aid of a liturgy; another finds our own simpler order more helpful to him. You are not going to help the kingdom by trying to bring about a forced uniformity of method and organization. Let each man work and worship in the way that suits him best. It will be the same Lord all the time that worketh all in all.

It would have been quite easy to prove that this attempt to enforce a rigid uniformity of thought and belief and method has been the greatest barrier in the way of human progress, but I pass that by in order to be able to dwell for just a moment upon the need for the assertion of individuality.

Assertion of Individuality

David declined to be an imitation Saul. Had he gone forth in Saul's heavy and unwieldy armor, you may be quite sure of this, there would have been no victory over Goliath. But he had the moral courage to refuse to be a feeble copy of Saul, and just to be himself. He put Saul's gorgeous armor aside, saying, "I cannot go with these; for I have not proved them." And David put them off him. When he went forth to face Goliath, it was with those weapons in his hand that were his own and that he knew how to use. "And he took his staff in his hand, and chose him five smooth stones out of the brook, and put them in the shepherd's bag which he had, even in his scrip; and his sling was in his hand, and he drew near to the Philistine" (1 Samuel 17:40). And David won his great fight that day just because he dared to be himself.

And that is what I would say to all who desire to be efficient workers and valiant fighters for the Lord—*be yourselves.* Give your individuality play. "Whoso would be a man," says Emerson in that great essay to which I have already referred, "must be a nonconformist"— nonconformist, I need scarcely say, not in the ecclesiastical sense, but in the sense—that no matter what the world may think or say, he will speak his own language, think his own thoughts, work on his own lines, and generally *be himself.* Be yourself! Be the man God meant you to be.

Work in your own way. We recognize in secular affairs that in choosing a calling or a business for a boy, consideration should be had to the bent of his own mind. The same principle holds good in higher things. It is not what the world—even the religious world— counts the correct way that matters; what matters is that every man should work in the way best suited for him. It matters little whether it is counted correct or orthodox. It is his way—let him work in it. Think what would have happened if certain men we know of had allowed themselves to be coerced into orthodox ways of work. If Francis had been coerced into recognized ways of service, there would have been no revival in Italy. If Luther had been coerced into living and working in orthodox monastic fashion, there would have been no reformation in Europe. If John Wesley had been coerced back into the respectabilities of Anglicanism, there would have been no evangelical revival or Methodist Church. If William Booth had allowed himself to be bound down by the red tape of Connexionalism, there would have been no Salvation Army. They did their great work because they dared to be themselves. Let every man follow their example. Be yourselves. Don't copy. Don't imitate. Work according to the law of your own being.

Think your own thoughts and believe your own beliefs. Hast thou faith? Have it to thyself before God. To thine own self be true. This is axiomatic—no man can fight effectively in the Christian warfare with borrowed weapons, with second-hand opinions and beliefs. The man who wants to speak effectively and work effectively in Christ's cause must have convictions that are his own, beliefs which he himself has proved. There is more power in the proclamation of one personal conviction than in the repetition of a score of borrowed and orthodox beliefs. David fared better with that sling of his and the five smooth stones from the brook—it looked a poverty-stricken equipment, it is true—but he fared better with it than he would have done had he gone into the fight clad in a complete panoply that was borrowed and not his own. It is much like that with our religious beliefs. The world is ready to supply us with a complete creed ready made. But such a borrowed creed will not be of much service.

I feel myself oftentimes I should like to have a complete theology, and I have textbooks on my shelves ready to supply me with one. But then I remember that the only beliefs that are worth preaching are the beliefs which are part and parcel of my own experience; the only truths that are worth proclaiming are the convictions of my own soul. So I turn away from the ready-made systems of the text-books. "I cannot go in them; I have not proved them." Beliefs which are to be effective are not borrowed; they are discovered, they are hammered out in life and experience. It is not the length of a man's creed that tells, but the conviction with which he holds it. And so I say, let every man think his own thoughts, believe his own beliefs, speak his own words. Let him be a voice and not an echo. Let him speak that which he knows, and testify what he himself has seen. All history tells us there is power for men, progress for the race, victory for the kingdom only when men rise clean above all fear of what the world may think or say and dare to be the men God meant them to be, to work in the way God meant them to work, and to speak the word God meant them to speak.

The Success of Individuality

Notice, in the last place, and in a sentence or two, what blessings followed David's assertion of his own individuality. I dare say Saul smiled when he saw David go forth with his sling and five stones. We know how Goliath mocked him and insulted him when he saw him approach. But we also all know the end of the story. David won a notable victory for Israel that day. And he won it by being David and refusing to be an imitation Saul. What we need to realize is that God wants all types of men in His service. He does not want all men to be of one type. He wants all types. He wants Saul to be Saul. He wants David to be David.

Look at the circle of the apostolate. What varying types you have there—Peter, the man of impulse; John, the man of strong enthusiasm; Andrew, the man of common-sense; Matthew, the man with literary gift; Philip, the man of affairs; Thomas, the man of gloomy but devoted heart. Our Lord did not try to convert them all into men of one type. He wanted Peter to be Peter, and John to be John, and Andrew to be Andrew, and so on. He needed the individuality of each. There was opportunity and work for each.

And so it is still. Christ wants you and me—as we are, with our individual capacities and gifts. We rob and impoverish God when we become feeble copies and imitators of somebody else. He has work for us, and He wants us as we are. Yes, even though we seem to have but little to offer him. Even though, like David, our only equipment be a sling and five smooth stones. God can do the most amazing things with weak and unpromising tools.

Think of D.L. Moody—he was the manager of a Chicago shoestore, without any education worth the name. He heard God call him, and he gave himself to God as he was. He gave his life to the service of his Lord and began to speak for Him. He never went to college; he never belonged to what is known as the regular ministry. I have no doubt many wished he had been trained and had taken "holy orders." But supposing D.L. Moody had done the orthodox thing and gone to college, the world might have gained an indifferent minister and lost the greatest evangelist of modern times. But he gave himself to God as D.L. Moody, the Chicago boot manager—with what many would think his very imperfect equipment—and God used him to quicken religion in two continents.

It is as we are that God wants us. With our poor sling and five stones, let us offer ourselves to Him. He can put His treasure in earthen vessels. He can and will repeat His ancient miracle; He will use the weak things of the world to put to shame the things that are strong, and the things that are not to bring to nought the things that are.

Opposition Is Opportunity

J. Stuart Holden (1874-1934), Vicar of St. Paul's Church, Portman Square, London, was an Anglican preacher of great ability. Possessing an engaging personality and persuasive manner, Holden was known on both sides of the Atlantic for his convention ministries. Holden was leader of the Keswick movement for almost 30 years and guided it ably. Skilled as a diagnostician of the deeper spiritual life, he helped guide many in discerning the difference between spurious and genuine faith.

This message on God's mercy is from *A Voice for God* by J. Stuart Holden, published by Hodder and Stoughton, London, 1932.

J. Stuart Holden

9

OPPOSITION IS OPPORTUNITY

An open door . . . and many adversaries (1 Corinthians 16:9).

THERE ARE THREE passages, fragments of the Holy Word, which I would ask you to conjoin in your minds, that together they may form a basis for the illustrative treatment of a subject of great consequence to all Christian people.

The first of them is in John 11:9. This, you recognize, is part of the record of Christ's journey to Bethany on the occasion of the sickness and death of Lazarus his friend. "Jesus answered, Are there not twelve hours in the day? If any man walk in the day, he stumbleth not, because he seeth the light of this world. But if a man walk in the night, he stumbleth, because there is no light in him. These things said He: and after that He saith unto them, Our friend Lazarus sleepeth; but I go, that I may awake him out of sleep."

The second is in 1 Corinthians 16:8, 9. This is a setting forth by Paul of the purposes he has in mind for future service. He says, "But I will tarry at Ephesus until Pentecost. For a great door and effectual is opened unto me, and there are many adversaries."

The third passage is in 2 Timothy 4:1-5. "I charge thee therefore before God, and the Lord Jesus Christ, Who shall judge the quick and the dead at His appearing and His kingdom; preach the word . . . But watch thou in all things, endure afflictions, do the work of an evangelist, make full proof of thy ministry. For the time will come. . . ."

Have these together in mind as I endeavor to speak on the general proposition that a man's spiritual opposition is ordinarily his spiritual opportunity. For if that truth only lays hold of us, that is, if we let it lay hold of us, there is not one of us who shall go hence to an unfruitful life.

If there is one thing the New Testament makes blindingly clear in regard to the Christian life, it is that from start to finish it only makes its predetermined way by overcoming a strong host of foes. According to the New Testament, the Christian life is no care-free, light-hearted, effortless saunter through sunlit spaces, with nothing to keep the mind and heart and will alert, with no threat, no menace, no challenge to its security and its enthusiasm. According to the New Testament, Christian faith proceeds upon its strong assurances, never upon its immunity from open attack and hidden pitfalls and insidious antagonism. For it enjoys no such exemption. On the contrary, it moves forward always in battle array. It wears its shining armor night and day. It needs to, for its enemies are many and strong and sleeplessly vigilant. It have well been said that the genius of the Christian life is not that it believes in spite of evidence but that it proceeds in scorn of consequence.

It was a true instinct as well as a faithful recording of the facts of experience that inspired a hymn much in vogue amongst us in earlier years. We have not gained by the loss of it from our modern hymn-books.

> Why should I complain of want or distress,
>   Affliction or pain? He promised no less.
> The heirs of salvation, He says in His Word,
>   Though much tribulation must follow their Lord.

The charter of the Christian's life and his competence for all its obligations, as well as his upholding certainly in regard to its outcome and its crown, is in the word of Jesus to His bewildered followers who thought that the Kingdom should immediately appear, who believed that lives pledged to goodness should be unmolested, untroubled, free from opposition: "It is enough for the disciple that he be as his Master" (Matthew 10:25). In our less thoughtful and less true moments, when unusually exalted by some favorable circumstance and passing emotion, we are sometimes led away into singing what of course is not more than momentarily true, and hence not really true at all: "I feel like singing all the time." But we are not in harmony either with what He told us or with what life actually brings home to us when we even think of the Christian life in such terms.

One of the most urgent lessons we need to learn is how to act when opposition to the gospel of Christ, and to ourselves because of the gospel of Christ and our identification with it, is unmasked and unavoidable; what to do in situations that spell conflict for us. This is especially pressing, seeing that any conduct of ours affects not ourselves alone but the interests of Christ's Kingdom, of which we are each pledged and responsible members. We may each count only one. But we each do count one. And that count is a vital count. Hence I bring you these three great passages of Scripture that cast light upon the problem of the Christian witness which is bound to draw upon itself opposition and hostility.

Christ Goes to Bethany

Take the first one, and listen to the disciples talking to Jesus.

"Master, You are surely not going down to Judea again! That is where they stoned You! Don't be rash! There is surely a limit to everything, even to Your kindly intention, and certainly to actions which unnecessarily expose You, and incidentally us also, to danger. We know how earnest and brave and fearless You are, but, Master, do use a little common sense about this! It cannot be wrong, on the contrary it is surely in the highest degree right, to exercise ordinary care and prudence about Yourself. In view of the mission You have declared and embarked on, Your life is far too valuable to be risked in another stone-throwing brawl with those hot-headed fanatics down there."

Listen now to the Master speaking back to them! I do not think my imagination runs me into irreverance.

"Stones? Did you say stones? Why, the threat of stones is the last thing that could deter Me! Until My work is done I cannot be touched by any stone. My friends, you are too short-sighted! Have you never heard that God can raise up sons from stones? Why fear them then? Don't you know that there are other things in Judea as well as angry opposition? There is a man who is sick unto death, and there are his two distracted sisters, and there are many people wondering what difference the faith that those three have learned from Me, and have confessed openly, is going to mean to them now that trouble has visited their home. And listen! There is a bigger conflict there than any one of you can understand. For Death, the great enemy, is there. And what happens there when I go and face him is going to affect the thought and faith and life of the world for all time. Don't be so short-sighted! Nor so faithless! Of course I'm going. Surely you know, by now, that there's only one place for Me—the place of My Father's will. There may be enemies there. There probably are. But that's just because it is His place for Me, and because His business is there to be done. So let us be going."

Jesus is giving them an illustration, such as they could neither mistake nor forget, of the fact that what looks like opposition, and indeed actually is opposition, is always an opportunity of serving the will of God uniquely. He is giving them an example that they might follow His steps when, in similar circumstances, they should be confronted and challenged in coming days. It was just part of their training in discipleship, to learn how to look upon adverse situations, how to interpret those situations in the light of God's eternal purposes.

The whole incident was intended to fortify the disciples against the days when they should stand, each of them an unarmed man, before a formidable and even a brutal world. It was meant to save them from holding back when prospects should be unpromising and menacing. It was directed toward helping them to realize that their first impression of a situation may be entirely erroneous and misleading; to enable them to look beyond the outward circumstance to its heavenly control; to impress upon them that courage, even reckless courage, and not self-protective caution, is the master virtue of vital Christianity; to make it plain to them that there is a saving of life which is the losing of it. And not only toward helping them but us also.

Paul Stays at Ephesus

Now consider Paul, who says in regard to what he enjoins upon his fellow disciples, "I have first myself received it of Jesus," Paul who declares he had learned Christ, who claims to have the mind of Christ. Look at Paul in a situation similar to that in which we have seen his Master.

He is writing to his friends in Corinth about his plans. He is on the point of undertaking another missionary journey, and it is his intention to spend quite a considerable time in the city of Ephesus. He is confirmed in his conviction that this is what the Master would have him do just because alone with the open door, which was probably the expressed desire of a few Christians in Ephesus that he should visit them, there were many adversaries who would have to be met there!

He knew all about them, and probably those to whom he wrote knew about them also. Perhaps better even than he did. There was Demetrius! And there were the Diana-worshipers! All of them bitter, hostile, moved to unscrupulous enmity by their vested interests. I think that most men describing the situation as Paul and his friends visioned it would never have described it in this way. They would not say, "The Lord has opened a door wide and effectual for me, AND there are many adversaries." They would more likely say, "But there are many adversaries." And they would solicit, if not the help of prayer on the part of those to whom they wrote, at any rate the flattering unction of their pity.

Not so Paul. He knew well what his Corinthian friends would say to deter him. So he forestalls them by asserting that the certain opposition at Ephesus corroborates to him this challenging opportunity of service as being divinely ordered. We can almost hear Paul saying:

"Opposition? But that is what I am for! That is what Christ saved me for! Conflict? But that is what I enlisted for! The fact that there is likely to be trouble is the hallmark of the open door! It assures me as to Whom has opened it! Of course I will take care, God helping me. But what am I to take care of? Of myself or my entrustment? You say to me, 'Paul, keep well out of harm's way. Your life is too valuable to be thrown away.' That may be well enough for some men, but not for me. If I am in Christ's way, how can I keep out of harm's way? They are practically synonymous, just one and the same thing!"

Now Paul had already experienced something of what adversaries could do to him. But he had also learned, which is far more important, what adversaries could not do to him. He knew, too, that if his witness and his work were not opposed by the great enemy it could only be because they were not worth opposing. And such a revelation as that could only send him to his knees in humiliation. For nothing could be worse than that he be but sounding brass and tinkling cymbal. That *is* a thing to be afraid of. But to fear the enemies of the Cross of Christ? Never! "Many adversaries"? What of it, so long as he was using his opportunity worthily? So long as he was making some inroad upon the kingdom of darkness by extending the kingdom of Light? So long as he did not permit the invasion of his own peace nor acquiesce in the embitterment of his own spirit by personal resentment?. . . . "The Lord hath set before me an open door, and there are many adversaries." That is one proof to me that it really is the Lord who has opened it. And that is why I am going!"

Paul did not seek needlessly to arouse opposition. No sensible man ever does that. To provoke hostility by boastful challenge—he would have regarded that as foolish presumption. But he declined to be overawed or overridden in his purpose by the certainty of its unavoidableness. Antagonism is, to Paul, the authentic confirmation of his Master's direction. What could a man like Paul do but follow it?

How characteristic that is of the man as he is disclosed to us. Having received Christ's commission, all he could say, like Martin Luther, who followed him as he followed Christ, was: "Here I stand! God help me, I can no other!"

Danger was only a spur to his courage. It did not occur to him that there could be an easier way than the way of loyal obedience, or that anyone constrained by Christ's love should even dream of taking an easier way even if it were available. For Christian discipleship is not a soft job, a perpetual picnic, a sort of religious entertainment. Self-protection and the kingdom of God had for Paul, as they have for all of us, simply nothing in common. The Lord had said at the beginning of his course: "I will show him how great things he must suffer for My name's sake" (Acts 9:16). And from that time onward fear of untoward consequence never moved him from his steadfast determination to be the messenger of Jesus Christ and the witness of His power to all men. His consecration was utterly uncalculating. Bear that in mind, my friend, as from this mountaintop of vision you move down to the valley of duty, where the high aims you have visioned and laid hold of have to be realized in daily discipleship, in unapplauded and possibly unappreciated self-sacrifice, in self-forgetting fidelity. And that in the teeth of the hostility of many adversaries. Follow him as he followed Christ!

Paul knew, too, that at Ephesus controversy would surely be forced upon him. He did not enter upon religious controversy lightly. No man who seeks to be Christ's disciple ever does. There is, indeed, every evidence that controversy as such was not at all to his liking; for he knew, what has always been the case, that when a man's religion runs to controversy it most often runs to nothing. But, mind you, there are worse things than controversy. There are harder things for a man of faith to do than to withstand some people to the face because they are to be blamed. One of them is to refuse a task, to side-step, because it incurs opposition and arouses antagonism and involves him in serious personal consequences. The lines of least resistance and greatest popularity are seldom if ever laid in the direction of Christ's pathway. And the "peace-at-any-price" man has no idea what the price will mount up to before it is fully paid. Personal concern levies an insistent blackmail upon spiritual loyalty until it utterly bankrupts it.

Paul's faith in Jesus Christ, to whom he owed literally everything, would never allow him to put himself before his privileged mission, even though it did mean controversy with many adversaries. Rather, he says, "What an opportunity of serving the Lord's interests there is in the opposition that awaits me at Ephesus!" For he is very sure of his gospel. And so the prospect even of controversy does not unnerve him. He is not out to win arguments, he is out to win souls. And he knew well, what many of us have had to learn by bitter disappointment, that you may win arguments and lose hearers. You may convince a man's mind, run him to a standstill in religious contention, silence him utterly, and at the same time alienate him from that purpose for which you were divinely brought into contact with him. That's what a lot of modern controversy does. Flaunting the name of religion, it is actually irreligious both in method and motive. And it scatters the men its perpetrators were meant to persuade.

Paul knew he had an unassailable right to proclaim things about God and Christ. For he has experience in proof. He could point to himself, without any unbecoming immodesty, as an illustration of the Great Salvation. He could say to a man who was inclined to argue and to refute his proclamations: "My friend, before you can explain Jesus Christ away you have to explain me away! I was a persecutor, a blasphemer, and injurious. But God had mercy upon me! Christ has saved me from the guilt and habit of my sins." So the glory of the opportunity, with its immeasurable possibilities, completely obliterated the menace of opposition and personal danger from his mind. Toward Ephesus he went. For him it was the only road on earth.

How different all this is from the Christian who today says, "Yes, I suppose there is an open door for the testimony and witness of Christ. And I suppose I should give myself more whole-heartedly to it. But really there are so many adversaries! What would happen to my business, my prospects, my social position, if I became too definitely identified with Jesus Christ? One must be careful not to jeopardize one's interests by being too aggressively Christian. There is such a thing as going too far; and, after all, moderation is a virtue."

I wonder how, one day, such a person will meet Him who, in the greatest issue in which a man can be involved, depended upon him? And how, one day, will such a person meet those whom he actually wronged by his timorous withholding from them of that which he held in trust? For when a man has that same right of personal Christian experience as Paul had, and that same responsibility to declare things about God and Christ, he has something more also. For he has not only the promises and precepts of the gospel to rely upon, but he has its potencies also. He has assurances of the divine partnership which lifts, or should lift, him above every consideration of personal consequence. Hostility should no more damp his ardor than it should embitter his spirit. Such a person can say with Paul, "I have been crucified with Christ . . . nevertheless I live, yet not I, but Christ liveth in me" (Galatians 2:20). That's the measure of his responsibility.

Suffer me to say this, my friends, that every defection from the life of costly, active witness is only achieved by quenching the Holy Spirit of God. And from this may the good Lord deliver us all! Look you out again upon that open door which calls to you in your family, in your business, in your college, in your congregation.

Then look in again upon your resources, and set your face toward Ephesus, realizing that your opposition is your opportunity!

Timothy Preaches the Word

Now lastly, in the third of those Scriptures to which I have referred you, Timothy is being urged to this same courageous loyalty to Christ as Paul exemplifies. Paul is laying him under the same charge as that by which his own life has been ruled. Timothy is to preach, reprove, rebuke, exhort, to do the work of an evangelist, to make full proof of his ministry. Paul tells him he is to be "a man of God," with all that that title implies. And then this is adduced as an incentive. He does not say, "Do these things and you will see perpetual revival, spectacular success, widespread fruitfulness!" Rather he tells him that indifference and seeming failure will wait upon his efforts. "The time will come," he says, "when they will not listen to you. When they will turn their ears away from the Truth. When they will prefer a more soothing message than that which you bring them! But this is part of your commission. And your opportunity is diminishing all the time. Every day it is just a little less than it was. So be instant in season, out of season!" From out of his own experience he warns him: "They may not persecute you, but they will often ignore you. They will reject the message and break the messenger's heart. For those who will certainly treat you so are the spiritual descendants of those who, if they had only known, would not have crucified the Lord of glory. They literally don't know. Now it is your privilege to enlighten them. Their very opposition to you is your opportunity. That you should be entrusted with a mission like that, with a post in the high places of the field, is a signal mark of the Master's confidence. It gives you the certainty of being in the true succession."

Let there be no mistake about this. The place of Christian witness is often a hard and lonely place. But it is under just such conditions, matching the confidence of your faith against the apparent hopelessness of your efforts, that your own personal life will most surely develop. You may not appear to make much of the work entrusted to you. But it will make you! The man you are to be will not emerge from the man you are except by hardness and conflict and by the overcoming of obstacles in the power of Him who neither dispenses with your personality nor suppresses it as you engage together in the holy warfare.

Look out, then, upon that open door! And get you through it in fellowship with Jesus Christ! Look at the adversaries through the opportunity. Don't make the fatal mistake of looking at the opportunity through the adversaries. And remember, now and always, that Christ our Lord does not ask us to do anything that He does not propose to undertake also with us! "Who shall separate us from the love of Christ!" Many adversaries? (Romans 8:35). "Nay. In all these things we are more than conquerors through Him who loves us!" (v. 37).

Clean, for Service

George Campbell Morgan (1863-1945) was the son
of a British Baptist preacher and preached his first
sermon when he was 13 years old. He had no formal
training for the ministry, but his tireless devotion to
the study of the Bible helped him to become one of the
leading Bible teachers of his day. Rejected by the
Methodists, he was ordained into the Congregational
ministry. He was associated with Dwight L. Moody in
the Northfield Bible conferences and as an itinerant
Bible teacher. He is best known as the pastor of
Westminister Chapel, London (1904-17 and 1933-35).
During his second term there, he had Dr. D. Martyn
Lloyd-Jones as his associate.

He published more than 60 books and booklets, and
his sermons are found in *The Westminister Pulpit*
(London, Hodder and Stoughton, 1906-1916). This
sermon is from Volume 3.

G. Campbell Morgan

10

CLEAN, FOR SERVICE

Be ye clean, ye that bear the vessels of the Lord (Isaiah 52:11).

THESE WORDS REVEAL a philosophy of service for the people of God. They define the responsibility which constantly rests on those who bear His name, that responsibility being indicated in the words, "ye that bear the vessels of the Lord." Moreover, they declare the conditions on which this responsibility may be fulfilled, that, namely, of cleanness in the full sense of that great word.

Bible history reveals the long conflict between two opposing principles, represented by two words, Babylon and Israel; the one standing always for self-centered life, and the other for God-centered life .

Background: Babylon and Israel

It is not for us to trace with any minuteness of examination the conflict between these two principles as it is revealed in the Scriptures. We may, however, call to mind the landmarks in the case of each. Babel, Babylon, Babylon the great, the mother of harlots. These words serve as indices, and cover the whole movement in the Bible. Over against them we may think of the landmarks on the other side, Abraham, Israel, and Jerusalem, coming down out of heaven from God for the establishment of the divine order in the world.

In the first case we trace a movement, based on rebellion against God's government, and issuing at last in uttermost confusion as the great word of the Apocalypse indicates, "Fallen, fallen is Babylon the great" (Revelation 18:2). On the other hand, we trace a movement based on loyalty to God's government and issuing at last in eternal steadfastness. The realization of the divine order among the sons of men is indicated in that word of the Apocalypse, "Behold, the tabernacle of God is with men, and He shall dwell with them, and they shall be his peoples" (Revelation 21:3).

Ever and anon in the history of the people of God as recorded in the Scriptures, they are seen yielding to the spirit of Babel, and always as a consequence sharing its confusion. The picture of Jehovah presented, when one takes this outline view, is of One who broods over His people, and forevermore attempts to woo them back toward Himself. He does that because by their complicity with the spirit of Babylon they injure themselves, and, infinitely worse, because by their complicity with the spirit of Babylon they injure the nations round about them.

In this prophecy of Isaiah, and especially in this part from which our text is taken, we find ourselves in the midst of this conflict, where the two principles are clearly evident. As a matter of fact, at this time Israel, as viewed by the prophet, was in actual captivity in Babylon. Yet there was evident among them a divine movement toward return to loyalty to God, and consequently toward establishment in their own land. It is impossible to understand this text without recognizing that it forms part of a greater whole. At the fifty-first chapter we have the commencement of the prophet's appeal, "Hearken to me, ye that follow after righteousness, ye that seek the Lord" (v. 1). There were among the people of God those who were following righteousness, who passionately desired it, and were seeking the Lord. As we read on we find that the people were aroused as the result of the prophet's appeal, and they lifted a cry to God in these words, "Awake, awake, put on Thy strength, O arm of the Lord" (v. 9). Then we come to the answer of God to the cry of the people. It is found in the opening words of chapter 52: "Awake, awake, put on thy strength, O Zion" (v. 1).

The people of God were captive in Babylon, I pray

you notice carefully the suggestiveness of it. The people who stood for loyalty to God, and ought to have borne that testimony to the world, were slaves in Babylon, which represented antagonism to the government of God. Yet amongst them in slavery were those in whom was the consciousness of all they were failing to do, and the sign after something nobler expressed itself in that prayer to God, "Awake, awake, put on Thy strength, O arm of the Lord" (Isaiah 51:9). To them the answer of God, if I may reverently put it into other words, was this, Why do you cry to me to awake? I am awake. I am not asleep. It is for you to awake and put on strength, and put on your beautiful garments.

Then follows the strange movement which chapter 52 describes. The prophet's vision is a remarkable one. He sees the people in their captivity, and he sees messengers crossing the mountains between Jerusalem and Babylon, and the burden of the cry of the messengers to the people in captivity is this, "Thy God reigneth" (v. 7).

It had seemed to these captive people as though God had resigned the throne of government, and they had said, "Put on Thy strength" (v. 1). His answer is, It is for you to put on strength, and the watchman on the heights, and the messengers that traversed the roads between Jerusalem and Babylon cried to the captives, "Thy God reigneth" (v. 7). That cry was answered by a great song of hope, and the people are seen preparing to leave Babylon and return to Jerusalem.

At last the call came, "Depart ye, depart ye, go ye out from thence" (v. 11). The captives were called to leave the place of captivity and to make their way again to the city of their established government. As they were about to obey, this solemn word was uttered, "Be ye clean, ye that bear the vessels of the Lord" (v. 11).

They had suffered through the Babel spirit, under the influence of which they had passed. They had passed into captivity to Babylon because they themselves had bent the neck to the spiritual conception of Babylon.

Now revival was beginning as the people began to sigh after God and proclaim His continued reign. They were turning back again to the place of blessing. On the eve of departure, the solemn warning was uttered, "Be ye clean, ye that bear the vessels of the Lord" (v. 11).

Foreground: A Guiding Principle

Such is the background. In the foreground is this clear enunciation of abiding principle. Those who bear the vessels of the Lord must be clean. Let us then quietly and solemnly consider the two thoughts already indicated; first, the responsibility of the people of God; and second, the condition on which they are able to fulfil that responsibility. That responsibility is suggested in the words, "Ye that bear the vessels of the Lord." The condition on which it is possible to fulfil that responsibility is indicated in the command, "Be ye clean."

This principle of responsibility is enforced from the beginning of Bible history, and has been enforced over and over again by the prophets and interpreters of the ages, and yet, as Christian men and women and as a Christian church, it is a principle we are always in danger of forgetting. The principle is that the people of God exist, not for their own sakes, but for the sake of the peoples who are not the people of God.

God's people are ever intended to be channels of communication, through whom He may reach others in blessing. Bible history does not exhaust the possible illustrations, but I am content to confine myself within this limitation. The keyword of God's communication to Abraham was this, I will bless you, and you shall be made a blessing. "I will make of thee a great nation . . . and in thee shall all the families of the earth be blessed" (Genesis 12:2, 3). As we watch the building up of that peculiar people—who are today scattered and peeled, but retain with singular and remarkable persistence their national loneliness, even though they no longer have a national constitution* —as we watch the growth

---

* Written long before the free state of Israel was established (publisher's note).

of that nation, we see God's method for reaching other nations. Israel today is a people scattered and peeled over the face of the whole earth, because they forgot the meaning of their making, and they failed to understand that they were created, not in order that God might have a people on whom He might lavish His love in forgetfulness of other peoples, but in order that they might become the instrument through which He would reach other peoples. An illustration of the principle outside that of the covenant people is found in this prophecy of Isaiah in the words of Jehovah concerning Cyrus, "I will gird thee, though thou hast not known Me" (Isaiah 45:5). Trace the history of all national life through the ages and the same principle is discoverable. God makes a nation for a purpose. The moment that nation becomes self-centered, there comes disaster; He destroys the nation He has made. As the nation He makes realizes its responsibility for all the rest He maintains its strength.

The principle is most remarkably manifest in the life of the church of God. The church is the depository of the treasure of God for the race. The church of God is not an institution which holds within itself treasure for its own enrichment. Said the great apostle, whose peculiar phrase, "my gospel," referred to the church, "I am debtor." I am in debt to men. In what did his debt consist? In that he had received the great evangel, in that he had perfect understanding of the provision of the grace of God for men, wrought out into his own experience. Not for his saving only was he saved, but in order that he might be the instrument through which God might reach other men for their saving.

To the church is committed a threefold responsibility. She stands for the manifestation of God to the world. She exists for the reconciliation of the world to God. She has within her fellowship the living means of grace. Some of you may say that is very high-church doctrine. It is the highest of the high, because it is the New Testament doctrine of the church. She stands first for the manifestation of God. Hear this great word of the New Testament, "Ye are an elect race, a royal priesthood, a holy nation, a people for God's own possession, that ye may show forth the excellencies of Him Who called you" (1 Peter 2:9). In other words, the church exists to manifest God. Not through the Word alone will the world find the Father, but through the Word incarnate in the lives of people who have been obedient to it. Only through those who share His nature can His name ever be known.

We bear the vessels of the Lord. The world can find its way to the Savior only through the church. Do not misunderstand me, I mean through the church's proclamation of this Evangel. If you take the widest outlook, you see at once what I mean. He cannot reach the heathen people save through the contact with them of His own people. I am neither attempting to discuss the economy of God or to account for it. I declare it as a fact revealed and demonstrated by experience. The world is not waiting for salvation because God is unready to save, but because the church is not wholly at His disposal to carry the message of salvation. Knowledge of God can come to men finally, fully, completely, only through the church. He has committed to us the responsibility of revelation. We bear the vessels of the Lord.

The ministry of reconciliation is ours. We fulfill it by the revelation of His love, the revelation of the meaning of His atoning work, and the revelation of the power by which He remakes humanity. All these things are committed to the church, and men can know them only through the church.

The means of grace are committed to the Church, the inspired Word for its interpretation, the sacred activities of worship for explanation, and, infinitely more, and without the more these things are of no avail, that service of pity and of power which brings life to the dead, love to those who are lonely, and light to such as sit in darkness. All the treasures of God are deposited with the church. I do not mean any organized ecclesiastical system, but the whole catholic church, made up of men and women who share the life of Christ and walk in the light He brings. We bear the vessels of the Lord.

The one message of God is that of love. God's love message is, that because He seeks the highest good of man He is the implacable foe of sin. All the vessels of the Lord under the old economy symbolized this truth and called for the perfection of humanity. The ministry of the church in the world is with this end in view, that the works of the devil should be destroyed, and the ideals of God realized.

I go back again to the simplest statement of the truth. The world can find God only through His people. Or let me make that statement in quite another form. The only use God has for His people in this world is that the world may find Him through them. The church of God exists today for the bearing of the vessels of the Lord, for the revelation of the truth concerning Him, the opening to men of doors to fellowship with Him. The great deposit of the church creates the great responsibility of the church.

Let us hear what this text suggests to us concerning the conditions on which the church may fulfill her responsibility. We need to hear them because a statement such as this must bring to us consciousness of our own failure. You speak to me of the indifferent city. I tell you the reason for it is the faulty church in the indifferent city. We cannot realize our responsibility without knowing our failure.

With that thought in mind let us listen to what the prophet said concerning the conditions on which the responsibility may be fulfilled. "Be ye clean" (52:11). It is a very simple word. It is a very searching word. The word itself of which the prophet made use is suggestive. Its first intention is that of clarifying through and through. It is a word which suggests the idea, not of water, but of fire; not of something which deals with the external, but of something that searches through and through. I have been very interested in tracing through the whole of the Old Testament the use of the word here translated *clean*. The result of that survey is this: I find that it is never used of merely ceremonial cleansing. There are other words used in that sense, but this one never. It always has reference to moral cleanness. When the psalmist says, "The Lord rewarded me according to my righteousness; according to the *cleanness* of my hands hath He recompensed me" (18:20); "Therefore hath the Lord recompensed me according to my righteousness, according to the *cleanness* of my hands in His eyesight" (v. 24); "With the *pure* Thou wilt show Thyself *pure;* and with the perverse Thou wilt show Thyself froward" (v. 26), he in each case uses the same word. Perhaps the verse that helps us most to see the force of this word is that mystical and symbolic word in Canticles (6:10),

> Who is she that looketh forth as in the morning,
> Fair as the moon,
> Clear as the sun,
> Terrible as an army with banners?

Clear as the sun, that is pure as the sun, clean as the sun if you so will, and the figure of that verse explains the real thought of the word *clean*; it means clarified as with burning heat.

"Be ye clean, ye that bear the vessels of the Lord" (Isaiah 52:11). Be ye of that fire nature in which no imperfect or impure thing can live. Be ye of that nature which consumes the unworthy, and purifies that which is worthy. Be ye of the very nature of God Himself, of whom it is written, "Our God is a consuming fire" (Hebrews 12:9). The great picture of the testing of the church's work in the Corinthian letter comes to mind in this connection: He shall try our work as with fire. If you will allow your imagination to help you, look at the great picture of the Christ which is given in the Apocalypse by the seer of Patmos, "His eyes are a flame of fire" (1:14).

With eyes of flame he glances over the work of the church. With what result? Watch the work. Some of it is burnt, destroyed; it shrivels and becomes dust, and is gone; all that is hay, wood, stubble. Some of it loses only its dross and flashes in beauty as the fire of His glance rests on it; all that is gold, silver, and precious stones. These are the things that live in fire. These are the things of the fire nature, even though when you touch them they seem to be cold. They are fire nature, for fire cannot destroy them. In the ancient prophecy is this remarkable word, spoken to the king of Tyre, "Thou hast walked up and down in the midst of the *stones of fire*" (Ezekiel 28:14), stones that live in the midst of fire.

If we read the word, "Be ye clean," as though it referred only to some ceremonial cleansing, and inculcated certain ceremonial ablutions, we have not caught the force of the prophet's meaning. You bear the vessels of the Lord. You are to be responsible for His revelation to men. You are the people among whom He has deposited the truth for which the world is waiting. "Be clean," be clarified as by fire, be such men and women as that there is nothing in you that fire can destroy. Be such men and women that all the things fire can destroy are destroyed in your own life. "Be ye clean."

Our word *clean* may mean so little when it ought to mean so much. That great Hebrew word of which the prophet made use, which is used with such marked carefulness in all the language of the seers and psalmists of long ago, is a word which suggests cleansing in its profoundest sense: cleanness from complicity with Babylon. You have been in captivity to Babylon. You are sighing after the higher and nobler. "Thy God reigneth." God is calling you back to the place and position of power. Leave Babylon behind you when you turn your back on Babylon. Do not carry with you as you come again to the place you have lost any of the spirit that destroyed you before. The emblems of the holiness of the Divine government must be borne by holy men. "Be ye clean."

Desertion and Drudgery

George H. Morrison (1866-1928) assisted the great
Alexander Whyte in Edinburgh, Scotland, pastored two
churches, and then became pastor in 1902 of the
distinguished Wellington Church on University Avenue
in Glasgow. His preaching drew great crowds; in fact,
people had to line up an hour before the services to be
sure to get seats in the large auditorium. Morrison is a
master of imagination in preaching, yet his messages
are solidly biblical.

From his many published volumes of sermons, I have
chosen this message, found in *The Return of the Angels*,
published by Hodder and Stoughton, London.

George H. Morrison

11

DESERTION AND DRUDGERY

Simon Peter saith unto them, I go a fishing (John 21:3)

WHEN THE FEAST of Passover was ended, the disciples
left Jerusalem for Galilee. It was there, amid the scenes
of tender memory, that Christ had promised to meet
with them again. One would have thought that having
such a promise they would have hurried north without
delay. We should not have expected them to linger in
Jerusalem, when it was in the highlands they were to
see their Lord. But we must bear in mind that it was
Passover, and that the disciples were believing Jews,
to whom it would have seemed impiety to quit the city
before the feast was ended. That was why they waited
for ten days, and only then set out for Galilee.

When they reached it, and its familiar scenes,
everything was as it had been in the past. Unruffled
by the tempest in the south, unshadowed by the
darkness of the cross, the simple life was flowing on as
usual, and the meadows were beautiful with lilies. After
the strain and agony of Calvary, that rural quietude
would be like heaven. There would be no thought of
instant labor, for any moment Jesus might appear. But
the days went on and the master did not come, and
every evening the fishing boats put out, until at last it
was too much for Peter, and he cried impulsively, "I go
a fishing." John would never have suggested that. Like
Mary, he had the gift of sitting still. But he saw the
wisdom of it when it was suggested, as did the others
of that little company, and it is on that resolve I want
to speak tonight. Will you follow me then while I handle
it in this way: first, there are seasons when Christ
seems to be lost; second, in such seasons duty still
remains; third, through duty lies the road to restored
fellowship.

The Lost Savior?

First, then, there are seasons when Christ seems to be lost. When the disciples went northward into Galilee, they traveled in the radiant hope of meeting Christ. It was not in their thoughts that they would have to wait; they were expectant of seeing Him at once. Before He was crucified Christ had told them that it was in Galilee that He would meet them. Then, lest perchance they had forgotten it, the angel in the grave repeated it. And as if to make assurance doubly sure, Christ Himself, on resurrection morning, charged the women to go and tell the brethren to go to Galilee, and they would see Him there. Three times the promise had been given, and they did not doubt it for a single instant. So they went northward eager with expectancy, saying, "Tomorrow we shall see the Lord."

When tomorrow came, and the sunshine lit the waters, and the smoke rose heavenward from cottage fires, no one moved into the village street having the marks of the nails upon His hands. Their thoughts were full of Him—that made it all the harder. Everything they saw suggested Christ. There was the very boat upon the beach in which He had preached one memorable day. So they woke and wandered by the shore, and spoke of the dear dead days beyond recall. Then the sun set, and the glittering stars came out, and nowhere did they have a glimpse of Jesus. They needed Him, and yet they could not find Him. They watched and waited, and He did not come. Their hearts sank within them and were heavy, and they looked at each other with despairing eyes. The sky was as blue as it had ever been, and the peace of God was sleeping on the lake; but for them there was no peace, no rest, no beauty, because the Lord they loved seemed to be lost.

Now no one here has seen Christ in the flesh, nor shall we look on Him with our eyes this side of the grave; yet in spiritual senses is it not true that there are seasons when He withdraws Himself? There are times when Christ seems absent from the world, and evil triumphs without hindrance. There are times when

Christ seems absent from the church, and its worship is only fashion or routine. And there are times when Christ seems absent from the soul. Then faith is dead, comforts are departed, and one is ready to cry again with Mary, "They have taken away my Lord, and I know not where they have laid Him" (John 20:13). It is then that one prays, and prayer seems a mockery. It is then that the Bible loses all its dew. It is then that one comes to church, and bows the head, with a heart that is a thousand miles away. And one is never glad in such a season. One is fretful, irritable, weak, and every today is but a makeshift, and the grasshopper becomes a burden. Such seasons are always hard to bear. They cast a shadow on the leafiest June. When we have known Christ and when we seem to lose Him, it takes the sunshine and the joy from everything. It is in such hours a man is prone to fall, and to clutch again at what he had forsworn. It is in such hours that, for a word of sympathy, a woman will bow down her head and weep.

May I say in passing to any in that state that there is a word of comfort for them here: Christ had withdrawn—He was not to be seen—yet was He watching the seven all the time. They looked for Him and He never came. They had His promise and He disappointed them. And they went out to fish and it was night, and they were unsuccessful and alone. And all the time, not very far away, standing upon the beach and watching them, was the Master whom they thought that they had lost. They were never more precious to Him than they were that night. They were never dearer to His heart. The future of the world was in that boat, and Christ in an agony of love was watching it. Yet they thought he had forgotten them, and they were dejected because they could not see Him. Perhaps they fancied that in angel company He was too mighty now for humble fishermen. I beg of you, then, not to misjudge Christ. When He seems lost, He is not far away. He is standing on the beach, within hail, when the net is empty and the heart is sick. Only it takes a little love to see Him, and to cry in the grey dawn, "It is the Lord" (John 21:7); and it takes a little courage to leap out, and make for His pierced feet upon the shore.

So far, then, upon our first head—there are seasons when Christ seems to be lost. Now a word or two upon the second—in such seasons duty still remains.

Duty Remains

When Simon Peter said "I go a fishing" (v. 3), you are not to regard it as a sinful impulse. It has been taken so, and by some eminent scholars, but I am quite convinced that they are wrong. It was not a counsel of despair. It did not mean that Peter was now hopeless. It was not a return to the old life in Galilee, as if the discipleship had been a dream. It was the action of a man of energy, to whom it was torture to be sitting idle, and who would fill in the hours till his Lord appeared by doing the plain duty at his hand. There were many things that Peter could not do. He was not a scholar, he was not a farmer. But there was one thing he could do, and do well—and it was not a great thing—it was fishing. That is Peter at his best, the man who was waiting to see his Lord again, and who in the meantime, when it was dark as night, went doggedly and quietly to duty. No one could have blamed these seven disciples had they wandered listlessly along the shore. They were unsettled; they were tossed and torn; they had a score of excuses for not working. But Simon Peter said, "I go a fishing"—there is work to do and I am going to do it. There was no joy for him—his Lord was absent—but the doing of his duty still remained.

Now that is a lesson we all need to learn, and it is not always an easy one to learn. Think, for example, of the time of sorrow. There are sorrows in human life so overwhelming that they seem to blot out the love of God. It is so hard to see the meaning in them—so difficult to discern the hand of pity. And life seems shattered into a thousand fragments, and summer shall never be so sweet again. How shall one pray when prayer has been mocked, the heart is empty, and the coffin full? It may be idle to talk of trust in God. That is the very thing that has been crushed. But at least you can rise out of an idle grief and say with this gallant heart, "I go a fishing." For there is still some duty you are called to. There is still someone who is in need of you; there is still some service in your power to render this very day. It is hard to take the cross up in the sunshine. It may be harder to take it in the night. But hard or not, that is what Peter did, and that is what you must do if you would triumph. For always that is the pathway to the music and to a peace more exquisite than music and to a trust in God that blossoms red, although its roots are in the silent grave.

Or think again of a young man who has won his liberty and lost his faith. He was nurtured in a Christian home, and he believed implicitly the Christian doctrine. He believed in it because he loved his mother. He came to church because his father did. And every night he knelt and said his prayers, as a little child he had been taught to pray. But now it is different—now he is a man—now he has begun to read and think. For a little, Christ has disappeared, and God is but the shadow of a shade. There is nothing to be proud of in that state. There is nothing to despair of in that state. Christ understands it—He has seen it often—He is not far away though He be hidden. But now, if ever, a man must rouse himself, cling to duty, and cleave to what is good. Now, if ever, like Simon Peter, he must cry to his comrades, "I go a fishing." He must be good however hard it be. He must be pure however keen the battle. He must believe, although the heavens are silent, that it is better to play the man than play the beast. He must struggle up the mountain in the night, and then, when the day dawns and it is sunrise, he will have such a prospect at his feet as will tell him that the climbing was worthwhile.

Duty Restores Fellowship

And so I reach the last truth I want to give you: Through duty lies the road to restored fellowship. It was when they had toiled, and toiled heroically, that they discovered Jesus on the shore. There is something magnificent in their persistence all through the weary hours of that night. Time after time their nets were shot, and time after time their nets were empty. Yet they held to it till every light was quenched that had been twinkling seaward from the village, and the only sound that broke upon the silence was the calling of the night-bird on the loch. The wonder is that they did not give it up. They must have been intensely disappointed. The fish were there, for other boats were taking them, and they were quite as skillful as the best. And yet they held to it all through the night, and till the dawn was crimsoning the east, and it was then that Jesus Christ came back. They did not find Him because of their success. They found Him because of their fidelity. He did not come after a day of triumph. He came after a night of toil. Not in despair, but from a sense of duty had Simon Peter cried, "I go a fishing;" and he discovered when the morning broke that duty was the road to restored fellowship.

My brother and my sister here tonight, may I impress on you that it is always so? When the gladness and the glory are departed, that is the way to come at them again. You cannot always walk upon the mountains. You cannot feel like singing all the time. We are so strangely wrought of soul and body that such exultancies are sure to pass. But at least you can say when darkness is around you, "Please God, I am going to be faithful;" and to you, as to Simon Peter on the lake, that will restore the vision by and by. It is sweet to pray when the gates of heaven are open.

It is sweet to serve when everyone is grateful. But I will tell you something that is not so sweet, and yet may be worthier in the sight of God. It is to pray when the heavens are as brass. It is to serve when nobody is grateful. It is to do one's work, and do it well, though there is not a star in all the sky. That is the way into strength of character. That is the avenue to inward peace. That is how men, victorious over moods, come to discover Christ upon the shore.

Any baby can say, "I go a fretting;" but Simon Peter said, "I go a fishing." He went fishing, and he toiled all night, but then there came the morning and the Master.

Submission and Responsibility

George Campbell Morgan (1863-1945) was the son of a British Baptist preacher, and he preached his first sermon when he was 13 years old. He had no formal training for the ministry, but his tireless devotion to the study of the Bible helped him to become one of the leading Bible teachers of his day. Rejected by the Methodists, he was ordained into the Congregational ministry. He was associated with Dwight L. Moody in the Northfield Bible conferences and as an itinerant Bible teacher. He is best known as the pastor of the Westminster Chapel, London (1904-17 and 1933-45). During his second term there, he had Dr. D. Martyn Lloyd-Jones as his associate.

Morgan published more than 60 books and booklets, and his sermons are found in *The Westminster Pulpit* (London, Pickering and Inglis). This sermon is from Volume 3.

George Campbell Morgan

12

SUBMISSION AND RESPONSIBILITY

I also am a man under authority, having under myself
soldiers; and I say to this one, Go, and he goeth; and to
another, Come, and he cometh (Matthew 8:9).

ALL THE SCENES of New Testament history lie in the
atmosphere of Roman government. Its earliest stories
are connected with the decree that went forth from
Caesar Augustus that the world should be taxed. The
last definitely historical picture that it presents is that
of a notable prisoner, at large in his own house in the
imperial city. As we read, we grow familiar with Roman
armies, with cohorts, legions, and bands; with captains,
centurions, and soldiers. We meet with seven
centurions.

Centurions on Parade

The first centurion appears in the passage from which
my text is taken; he came to Jesus about his servant
who was sick. The next one we see, at the close of the
gospel narrative, is in charge of the crucifixion of Christ.
Then, in the book of Acts we find Cornelius, a devout
man, the first Gentile believer to be baptized by the
Hebrew apostle. Next we read of a centurion placing
bonds upon Paul, and, as Paul objects, immediately
seeking the advice of his superior officer. Also, there
are the two centurions who were taking Paul to Felix
and protecting him from the threatened hostility of the
crowd. Another centurion took charge of Paul and gave
him great indulgence by the direction of Felix. Then,
at last we come to Julius, who was Paul's custodian on
his voyage, and who became interested in Paul, so much
so that he saved him from death at the hands of the
soldiers in the hour of threatened shipwreck.

In all these centurions there is something to admire; in some of them much to admire; and in one of them at least everything to admire. The three first mentioned stand out upon the page of the New Testament, and are remarkable in many ways. This one came to seek the aid of Christ for his slave, and uttered the remarkable words of my text. At the crucifixion another centurion watched the dying of the Man of Nazareth, and so keen and accurate was his observation that he said, "Truly this was the Son of God" (Matthew 27:54). Of Cornelius the highest things are written.

In Search of Excellence

How is this excellence to be accounted for? If I were to declare that the military system accounted for it, I am inclined at once to say that would be too broad a statement, yet there is a sense in which it is true. I want to discover that sense, and to make it the method of my appeal to the young manhood of this congregation, to whom this message is to be particularly delivered. The end of the life of the soldier is not in view. I am not dealing with that. Whether that end be war, or whether it be that for which war is waged, I am not discussing that question at all at the present moment. It may be that if I were I should arouse the hostility of some of you, or, rather, I should not find you in perfect agreement with my own standpoint. I think there is a wonderful amount of insight in words that occur in *The Comments of Bagshot*, "There is no peace at any price party. There are only various parties which disapprove of each other's wars." I was recently reminded that so eminent a theologian as the late Dr. Dale once said, "I am for peace at any price, even at the price of war if necessary." I am not discussing that. I am attempting to bring you to a consideration, not of the end of the soldier's life, whether that end be war, or the reason for which war is waged; but of the method of the soldier's life. In understanding that method, we shall discover why it is that these men of the old Roman armies had an excellence that attracts us.

That method is declared clearly and simply and inclusively in the words the centurion uttered to Jesus, "I also am a man under authority, having under myself soldiers" (Luke 7:8). That is a philosophy of life. I wonder if he had ever said that before. I think not. I am inclined to think that it was a sudden expression of a subconscious philosophy. Remember, while he spoke in the first person singular, and while the philosophy was stated in the terms of experience and not in the terms of theory, this declaration was drawn from him by what he saw in Jesus. With an accuracy that should make us very thankful, the revisers have restored to the text a little word omitted in the Authorized Version, "also." You can drop the word "also" and you still have the philosophy, you still have the experience. "I am a man under authority, having under myself soldiers." That is my whole text, and yet it is not my whole text. It is the "also" that attracted me to the text. It is the supreme word. The centurion implied that Christ was a Man under authority and that He had those under Him. He looked at Christ and he saw in Him the fulfillment of the highest ideal of life as He knew it, and so Christ compelled from him the confession of the level upon which he was living his own life, the confession which revealed the philosophy of his life, which I think he had never formulated before.

The Philosophy of Submission

I shall ask you, first of all, to consider this philosophy of life, "I am a man under authority," that is submission: "having under myself soldiers"; that is responsibility. I am a man under authority. I have soldiers under me. I know how to bend the knee to a throne. I am able to exercise the power of a throne. I have kissed a scepter. I sway a scepter. I am responsible to a throne. I therefore am able to be responsible for those who are beneath me. I am a man under authority, submission. I have soldiers under me, responsibility. That is the highest philosophy of life that can be stated for a young man.

Let us attempt to see a little more clearly what it really means. So far, then, as the method of the life of the centurion is concerned, I borrow the career of one who is the ideal for young men. First consider the view of life suggested, and then see how the Christian life realizes that ideal at its highest and best.

What is this view of life suggested? This man first said, "I am a man under authority." To illuminate this I will take three simple prepositions: "to," "of," "for." "I am . . . under authority." That is submission to, submission of, and submission for.

Submission to. The Roman soldier was submitted to the cause of the Roman Empire, but for the Roman soldier the cause of the Roman Empire was personified in the emperor. The Roman soldier was under authority, so he was submitted to a cause personified in a person. You need not stay with the Roman soldier. It is true all through the ages. "For king and country" is the motto of the soldier today. The king is the personification to the soldier of the larger purpose and issue. The soldier is submitted to the cause of his country as it is personified for him in the king.

Submission of. The submission means submission of the central will. Upon enlisting in the army of the emperor, the Roman soldier surrendered his will, his property, his relations. From the moment when he enlisted he had no will of his own, no possession of his own, no property of any kind. He could not hold property. Neither could he speak of his relations as any longer being his. He gave up everything. The soldier submitted to a central authority has submitted his will and everything else. His time, his habit of dress, his choice of foods, and all his ability are handed over.

Submission for. The Roman soldier was submitted for fitting himself for his work. That meant drill. He was submitted also for his work. That meant war.

The centurion was submitted to the service of his country personified in a sovereign; he had made submission of his will and of all he had: he had submitted for the purpose of his own perfecting, for the accomplishment of the work to which he was called.

Turn to the other side of this: responsibility, "having under myself soldiers." I want you very patiently to follow me as I say that the responsibility of the centurion was connected intimately with his submission. He was responsible for the soldiers under him, to the state to which he himself was submitted. He must identify himself with them. He must exert an influence upon them. He must insist upon certain things in their lives. All this for the sake of the state. The state looked to him and held him responsible for all those who were placed under him, that he should recommend it, utter its requirements, and insist upon the realization of its purpose.

There was the most intimate connection between the soldier's submission and his responsibility. "I also am a man under authority, having under myself soldiers." The first was an upward look to the throne to which he bent; the second was a downward look to the territory over which he reigned. The upward look was in order that he might realize the territory over which he reigned. The downward look was in order that he might satisfy the throne under which he served.

In order that we may understand this great philosophy of life, I am more anxious that we should realize the connection between these two things than that we should see either in isolation. This is not a picture of the two sides of a man's nature, the one side subservient to authority, and the other getting satisfaction out of the fact that he was able to make others bend the knee to him. Here is a man who says, "For seven years I have been serving a master, now it is my turn. I am going to make someone else serve me!" Or here is a man who says, "In a certain department of my life I have obeyed; now I am going to compensate myself for the irksomeness of that by making someone else obey me." That is not the picture presented by these words. Let us be careful to draw the distinction.

The unifying conception of life to the centurion was the Roman Empire. He said, "I am under the empire and of the empire. I submit to its authority and I represent its authority. I look up to a throne in order that I may represent the will of the throne to those over whom I reign. I look down upon the territory over which I reign in order that I may realize in it the will and purpose of the throne to which I am submitted. This is a perfect harmony and interrelationship. There can be no right and perfect government of the territory over which I reign, save as I am in right relationship to the throne over me. The reason I should perfectly submit to the throne over me is that I may exert its influence among those who are placed under me. I am under authority, submission; I have soldiers under me, responsibility. The responsibility of reigning is intimately connected with submission."

The Application of Submission

That is a revelation of perfect life. Before I turn to show that the Christian ideal realizes that, do you see the importance of it? Let me get my sermon out of shape and take the application now. To what throne is your life submitted? What territory are you reigning over? Have you found a throne to which you bend the knee? Have you found a throne to which you reign? That is the meaning of human life. Every man is intended to reign, but before a man can reign he must submit. Every man here has found a throne. Every man has found a territory over which he is reigning. You cannot escape it. These are the deep things of human nature which no man can elude. The trouble is that men submit to the wrong throne, and therefore their reign is that of despotism, destruction, death.

The influence you are exerting within the circle of your own manhood, the circle of your friends, in your home, your city, is an influence created by your relation to a throne. If the throne before which you bow is the throne of the world, or the throne of the flesh, or the throne of the devil—and these are not separate thrones, that is the trinity of evil—if you bow before that throne, you are still reigning, but it is a reign of devastation, a reign of death. You cannot escape submission to a throne. You cannot escape the exercise of influence, of power. Whether the power be constructive or destructive, for life or death, for lifting or flinging down, depends upon the throne to which you bow the knee. Every man can say, "I also am a man under authority, having under myself soldiers." I am not here to press young men to go forth and find a kingdom. I am here to press them to see to it that they find the right authority, and are exercising the right influence in the place where they reign.

The Pattern of Submission

That leads me to the second point. The Christian revelation most perfectly realizes this ideal of life. That ideal was perfectly presented as a pattern in Christ. That is what this man meant, though I do not imagine, or suggest, that he perfectly understood it. Thou art a Man under authority, and Thou hast soldiers under Thee. That is the story of Christ's life. Jesus of Nazareth might have said with perfect accuracy and with far fuller, richer, more spacious meaning than did the centurion, "I am a Man under authority, having under Myself soldiers." Jesus Christ was under authority. He was under authority to the state, the great universal empire of God, which He expressed in that term which we are still using and are only beginning to understand the meaning of, "The Kingdom of God." That for Him was personified in God Himself, Who was King, Ruler, Sovereign over the whole empire. He was a Man under authority. "I do nothing of Myself . . . I do always the things that are pleasing to Him" (John 8:28,29). "My meat is to do the will of Him that sent Me, and to accomplish His work" (John 4:34).

Christ's was a life under perfect and absolute authority. It was a life of perfect and absolute submission. It was a life, therefore, responsible, "having under Myself soldiers," all the forces of the Kingdom of

God over which He was appointed to reign. He was under authority and exercised authority. The authority He exercised over the things under Him was the authority to which He submitted, as He yielded Himself wholly to the will of God. The authority of life, light, love, the authority of pure, high, noble ideals; to these things He yielded Himself, for they were in the will of God. These are the very elements of the empire of God. Wherever He exercised His authority it was toward the realization of these things in human life.

Christ did not merely reveal to us the fulness of this ideal as a pattern; He came to call us into submission to it, and to communicate to us the power that would enable us to fulfill that in our life, which is essential to it on the highest level and in all fulness and breadth.

The Call to Submission and Authority

To what, then, does Christianity call every young man? To submission and authority! Submission to what? To the Kingdom of God personified in Christ as King. I call you in the name of this Christ to submission to the Kingdom of God. I pause because I am so conscious that the familiarity of these terms robs them of their spaciousness and grandeur and beauty. Young men are constantly telling me they are looking for a career. Here is an all-inclusive one, passion for the Kingdom of God. All honor to the soldier who really and truly and deeply loves his country. I ask you to make the master passion of your life not this country of Britain, but the Kingdom of God. If the idea be too spacious, too gracious, as indeed it is, then focus it, localize it, personify it, only remember that when you have personified it, that to which you come, or He to whom you come, does stand for the larger purpose, the Kingdom of God.

We call you for this purpose to the Christ, for submission to Him is submission to the Kingdom of God. Come, not merely that you may kiss a scepter and be under a King, but that you may make the

Kingdom of God the goal of your endeavor, the passion of your life, that to which you devote all your energies. Here is the true throne. Here is the true state. Here is the true empire to which men should give themselves. The man who can go forth from this chapel saying, I am a man under authority to God's King and God's Kingdom, is fulfilling the essential necessity of his life on the highest level and in the fullest, best sphere.

The Reality of Submission

Remember that if submission means submission to the Kingdom of God it means submission of the will. As the Roman Centurion in the olden days, having handed over his will and choice, ceased to have property or time or relations of his own, so must the soldier who submits to the Christ. If you say I am carrying my figure too far, listen to the King Himself. "If any man would come after Me, let him deny himself, and take up his cross, and follow Me" (Luke 9:23). "If any man cometh unto Me, and hateth not his own father, and mother, and wife, and children, and brethren, and sisters, yea, and his own life also, he cannot be my disciple" (Luke 14:26). This does not mean that the man giving himself to the Christ is to have no love for father, mother, wife, child, brother, sister; but that forever, in every hour of crisis, in every commonplace, in all circumstances, if there should arise conflict between the interest of Christ and that of father, mother, wife, child, brother, sister, Christ must have the pre-eminence, and the Kingdom of God must be first. So that "he that loveth father or mother more than Me is not worthy of Me" (Matthew 10:37) is the awful and yet necessary word of the King as men come into contact with Him and desire to submit themselves to Him.

Sometimes I think that we lose something of power and force by stating the case in all its widest reaches and its most spacious applications. It means that the soldier is to have no habit unremitted to Christ for approval or disapproval, no hour of his time which he calls his own, no interest in life which is to him vacation from vocation, no single detail of life over which Christ is not supreme, which does not enter into the supreme master passion of bringing in the Kingdom of God. That is the life of the Christian. I know there are a great many people who call themselves Christians who have never come within a million miles of realizing this. Are they Christians? I suggest the question and leave them to their own conscience and the clear teaching of Christ for decision. "Under authority." You have played at life long enough. Begin to live by giving yourself in tremendous submission to this King.

When you have done that, what then? Begin to reign in power. Begin to realize your kingdom. "Where shall I begin?" says some young man. "Give me my work." I give it to you now. "He that ruleth his spirit is better than he that taketh a city." That is in Proverbs (16:32). I am not going to preach from that text apart from the New Testament. I long ago gave up preaching the doctrine of self-control. I never say to a man, Control yourself. "The fruit of the Spirit is...self-control" (Galatians 5:22, 23). You begin to control yourself only as you hand yourself to your King. That is the first empire over which man is called to reign: All forces and conditions of his own life, the desires and aspirations; the movements of intellect, emotion, and will. I can reign only when I am under authority, when I have kissed the scepter.

Enlarge it without my staying to illustrate it. Your home, your class in the Sunday school if you are a teacher. This pulpit is a throne of power for me if I am under authority. If I am not, then it is an awful opportunity for wrecking human life. I am not talking idly. These are the deep and awful and heartbreaking convictions of any man who knows what it is to be called to preach the Word of God. Yet blessed be God, as the apostle declares, the true minister is "led in triumph." If I would reign in this pulpit and bring a territory into subjection to the vast empire of God's

Kingdom, then the measure in which I submit is the measure in which I command, and reign in my own life of service. So also in your city, in your country, everywhere. First under authority, and then reigning in power.

What Is Your Authority?

I go back to the application which I have already used in the middle of my sermon. Under what authority are you living? What are the sanctions of your life? To what do you remit everything? The lusts and desires of your own life? Is that so? Under what authority are you living? Tell me that, and I will tell you the effect you are producing upon the territory over which you are reigning. The authority to which a man submits is the authority he exercises. Let us break this up. Are you submitting your life to the authority of the flesh, answering its clamant cry, yielding all the forces of your being to whatever your flesh life asks and demands? Then you are exerting the authority of the throne to which you bow. You are spreading a poison and paralysis wherever you go for no man liveth unto himself. Are you bending the knee to the world with its maxims and methods? Then you are exerting the influence of the world in the circle of your friendship, and your friend is becoming worldly because you are reigning over him in the power of the world to which you bow the knee. Are you serving the devil, the devil who was a liar from the beginning and a murderer, the devil who is the prince of compromise and of subtlety? Then you are exerting the influence of the devil wherever you go. Are you serving that great Kingdom of God by crowning Christ? Then you are exerting the influence of that Kingdom and that Christ wherever you go. That which you are under, you transplant into that which you are over. That has a wider application than to young men. Fathers and mothers, that is true of you. It is not the precept which you utter, it is the throne before which you bend that you will see reproduced in your children. It is true everywhere. Let me cease my illustrations and leave the vast, awful sublime truth upon your conscience, and turn to my final word to young men.

A Word to Young Men

Young men, you must fulfill your manhood by bowing the knee to a throne and reigning. To what throne are you bowing? That life of yours, the history and mystery of which I know not, nor could I know if you attempted to tell me, the history and mystery of which you know not, for there are vaster reaches in your manhood than you have ever discovered. God only knows it all. Take that life and hand it over to that One who out of the eternal ages came into the little spaces of passing time that evil men might know the meaning of life in its richest fulfillment. Hand your life to Him and He will—this is the gospel, the evangel that comes like music to the heart of the man who has failed—He will "restore to you the years that the locust hath eaten" (Joel 2:25). He will give you back the things you have missed. Though the vessel be marred in the hand of the Potter, He will make it again, another vessel that seems good to Him. If you, like Jonah, in unutterable folly have paid your fare to try to escape Jehovah and have gone to Tarshish, if only you will get back, the Word of the Lord will come to you the second time, and He will establish His Kingdom in your life and then you may begin to reign in life.

Is there anything you more desire than a sense of power? Is there anything any man who is a man at all desires more than to be able to say, "I can"? It is the next great word to "I am" on the level of human life. "I am" is the first expression of human personality. If the next be "I think" the outcome is "I can." Do you want to say it? Oh, the scores of men who say to me, "I cannot." They are here tonight. You are here tonight, my brother, you are saying, "I cannot, God knows I would if I could, but I cannot do it. I see the vision, but

I have no virtue to win the victory." No, you have bent to the wrong throne, and the influence resulting from your bending to the wrong throne has been destruction of the territory over which you reign, for, remember, your paralysis is your own doing, your weakness is the result of your own yielding. I pray you turn the deafest of deaf ears to the false and damnable teaching that declares that you cannot help your sin. You can help your sinning. Sin is the rebellion of your will, and it is rebellion against God. You know that you need not have crossed the threshold of the house of sin, or put your life at the disposal of evil things; but you have done it and now you cannot help it, you are poisoned, paralyzed, spoiled. You are saying, I cannot, and you have ruined your kingdom because the throne to which you bent was the wrong throne.

There is a "trysting place where heaven's love and heaven's justice meet," and the trysting place is the cross where the Christ, who came to give the pattern, died that you might know how, in the mystery of pain, God is able to communicate power that makes life over again. If you have been the slave of the awful evil things to which you have yielded yourself, the chain can be broken now. God help you to find the right authority and bow under it, and so find your kingdom and reign over it.

SCRIPTURE TEXT INDEX